To my prophetic sons and daughters,
Hear the Word of the Lord. Speak the Word of the Lord.
Receive the Word of the Lord.

Scripture References: Unless otherwise indicated, Scriptures are taken from THE HOLY BIBLE, KING JAMES VERSION Copyright © 2020 by Holman Publishers. Nashville, Tennessee. Used by permission. All rights reserved worldwide.

Cover design by JIS Enterprise
Cover photography by Jeffery Rolle, JSR Photography
Editing by JQ Editing Services
Interior Formatting by www.queekpub.com
ISBN 13: 979-8-218-11496-1

Printed in the United States of America

DAILY PROPHECIES

Blessed be the Lord, who daily loadeth us with benefits, even the God of our salvation. Selah. *Psalms 68:19*

Mother,

When I was a little boy you taught me your God. You taught me that God would make a way out of no way. You taught me that if I trust Him, He would come through for me. Your faith in your God is remarkable.

I've seen you endure numerous battles and come out with the victory; all because of your faith in your God. I've watched you pray your family through difficulties, time after time. We were all amazed at how you championed hardships with only faith. You needed no other evidence except to believe. And time after time, your God always came through for you.

You called upon your God when we got sick. You anointed all of your household and the occupants with oil. You trusted your God when you purchased cars, homes, clothes, food, or an amazing Christmas. It was nothing too small or too great for you to trust your God for. That is the God you taught me to serve. That is the God you taught me to love.

I watched you trust your God when your body began to fail. I watched you trust your God when you were in pain and you simply said "Alright Mr. Jesus, c'mon today". And Mr. Jesus always came through with enough strength for you to make it through the day. Even when it seemed like He wasn't answering you, you trusted Him still. It was amazing to watch you decline but you kept believing and trusting your God. You didn't always trust Him to bring you out of it, you trusted your God to keep you through it. Your praise and faith remained constant and high even when things were the toughest for you. This only intrigued me more and more about this God you serve.

Today, I'm beginning to know your God the way you knew Him. I don't need much these days, just what He has willed for me to have and I'm alright with that. I'm beginning to trust your God more and more. I saw you do it, so I believe I can too. I pray often for your kind of faith. I ask your God to help me through. Not having you physically here can be debilitating at times. I too now find myself getting up some mornings and saying "Alright Mr. Jesus, c'mon today"

Thank you for telling me about your God. Thank you for leading me to your God. Thank you for introducing me to your God. For that I am eternally indebted and grateful to you. It's your God that I serve. It's your God that I love. It's your God that I have committed my life to. It's your God that I hear speaking in my ear. Your God has become my God.

#GWENDASGOD

✦ CONTENTS ✦

GOD'S INTENTION FOR NUMBERS

In Isaiah 40:28, the prophet asks hypothetical questions to point us to our innate inability to really know God. *"Hast thou not known? Hast thou not heard, that the everlasting God, the LORD, the Creator of the ends of the earth, fainteth not, neither is weary? There is no searching of his understanding."* Our attempts, though great to us are still a miniscule expression of the fullness of who God really is.

In humanities rigorous search to know the fullness of God, we have come up with names and titles to describe Him in ways that will agree with our limited comprehension. Some of these labels are based upon how God himself defines or describes himself. Other names have been attributed to God by our personal experience with God. These descriptions both attempt to define who God is and describe what He does.

For instance, if we examine the "Omni's" of God we will see an earnest effort made to reveal who God is. The prefix *omni* means all or absolute. This is a great foundation to begin to define God being that He is absolute in His existence. Meaning there is no fragments or partiality in the existence of God's being. To say that God is Onmipresent is to say that He is all-present or everywhere at the same time. There is no spot in the entire world, the universe, the cosmos, or the heavens that God does not exist. He is everywhere. God passes Himself on His way to where He just left. To say that God is Omniscient is to say that God is all-knowing. God cannot be shocked or surprised. He always possesses all information on all matters. God is the supreme intelligence on everything. To say that God is Omnipotent is to say that God is all-powerful. God does not need to recharge. He does not need to plug into anything to be refueled. God is not dependent on anything or anyone to exist. He is the source of all powers and power itself plugs into God to become powerful.

These are just a few descriptive labels we must utilize to further understand God. Another great name of God from the Hebrew language is Elohim. This is the name of God used in the book of Genesis when God created the heavens and the earth. Elohim is plural which would suggest that God is pluralistic in existence though He is singularly God. Though the name also describes other deities, when the Hebrew people used it, they are describing The only God who creates and is living. He is the creating God. He creates all things.

For this book, I want to lean into this name of God, Elohim. I want to talk about the God who creates. He created the earth we live on. He created the sky, the clouds, the trees, the mountains, the land, and crop. He created the waters, the ocean, and the seas. He created all living things. He created you and I and everyone who is living, who has lived and who will be born. God is the creator of all of it. Nothing created itself. Everything has origin in the mind of God and by the hands of God.

Revelations 4: 11 says *"Thou art worthy, O Lord, to receive glory and honour and power: for thou has created all things, and for thy pleasure they are and were created."* This text reveals that not only did God create all things, but also, He did it for His pleasure. Sometimes we overlook the small things in our life and forget that God created even those things. That favorite shirt you love to wear, God created the cotton from the crop or silkworm that was used to form that shirt. The wheat that was grown in the earth that was eventually made into flour made them pancakes you love to eat, and that sugar came from that sugar cane that grew in the field. The cocoa bean for the coffee you drink and the milk from the cow are all creations of God. Yes, God even made your breakfast. I know you were in the kitchen flipping those fluffy flapjacks, but had God not made the ingredients to make them, there would not be much of the morning delights that you love so much.

Another seemingly insignificant creation of God is numbers. While humanity often attempts to take the credit, it was God who produced the idea, concept and origin of numbers. God created numbers and He did so placing His stamp of similitude within the numbers He created. Firstly, there is an infinite amount of numbers. This is the same attribute of God, being that He is infinite, He never ends. Numbers are just like God. Also, like God, each number has a significance and meaning. God is noteworthy in all He does and is. God does not haphazardly create things with a certain amount nor is He random with how much or how little. God is intentional. When He made man on the sixth day, that was not by mistake nor was it arbitrary. It was intentional to reveal the character of the man in the character of the number six. All numbers have a significant character trait, which was created all by God.

Natural numbers are symbols or units that are part of a calculating and counting system. A number also stands for a position or amount in a series.

A number is different from numerals. A numeral is a representation of a number. The Egyptians invented a numeral system, which was improved by the Greeks. The Romans created the Roman numerals, using the Roman alphabet. In the late 14th century, the Hindu-Arabic numeral system became the most common system used around the world to represent the numbers. It is considered the most effective because of the symbol" zero." This is where we get the shape and form of numbers from. Many people take numbers for granted because they have always been there. However, for several cultures, the meaning of numbers follows age-old traditions and cultural beliefs.

The Chinese consider the number four an unlucky number since its Chinese pronunciation sounds like the Chinese term for" death." Therefore, buildings in China do not have a fourth floor. Well physically they do, but in the buildings' elevators, number 4 is not included. Instead, they use the letter F. The same belief is true in Japan and South Korea, and other Asian countries where Chinese is spoken.

But the belief is not applicable to Germany where the number is considered lucky, because it is associated with the" four-leaf clover" which is a symbol for luck.

In many countries around the world, including developed countries such as Norway, Sweden and the UK, the number 13 is considered an unlucky number. There is no accepted proof that the number 13 is unlucky, but it remains a sign of bad luck due to traditional beliefs. The Italians consider it a lucky number, as it is associated with Saint Anthony, who is the patron saint of finding lost people and things. Colgate University in Hamilton, New York significantly honors number 13 as the university was founded by thirteen men with a capital of $13. The school has thirteen articles and 13 prayers. Numbers are significant to many cultures and for many reasons.

Among the Jewish culture there is a code of numbers called the gematria. It is the Hebraic form of numerology in which the letters of the Jewish alphabet are substituted with corresponding numbers. In Hebrew, gematria is often used as an alternative to Arabic Numerals when recording numbers. Hebrew dates are written using gematria.

Numbers were created by God and have their origin of significance within Him, their creator. Elohim is the original and perfect numerologist. Please note that numbers are not to be worshipped. Many of these cultures reverence numbers as god or deities. But once again, Romans 1:25 states, *"Who changed the truth of God into a lie, and worshipped and served the creature more than the Creator, who is blessed for ever. Amen."* We are not to worship or serve numbers, however they are significant and noteworthy because their existence points back to God. To know numbers and their meanings, one must go to the Holy Scriptures and search the heart of God for the significant of all numbers.

In this book I will speak prophetically to you each day using the number of the day. Each number has a meaning that was originated in God, and it can speak to us if we pay close attention to it. Because God is Elohim, God will use the number to speak to you each day. Each date has a purpose and God brings each date in your life to speak to you and reveal to you His will for your life. This is not a horoscope nor is it an astrological approach to spirituality. It is God himself using what He has created (numbers) to speak to humanity.

OUR GREGORIAN CALENDAR

While we are taking a close look at the numbers for this book, I also want to explain to you how we got the calendar that we presently use. This will help us to understand deeply when each date arrives and the prophetic significance of that date. Our present calendar has deep roots into Christianity.

The Gregorian calendar is the calendar used in most of the world. Pope Gregory XIII, as a minor modification of the Julian calendar, introduced it in October 1582. Pope Gregory was a reformer in the Catholic Church. He is noted for his formation of the clergy and the promotion of the arts and sciences. He is mostly known for adjusting the calendar to ensure the Easter celebration falls in the proper season.

There were two reasons to establish the Gregorian calendar. First, the Julian calendar assumed incorrectly that the average solar year is exactly 365.25 days long, an overestimation of a little under one day per century. The Gregorian reform shortened the average calendar year by 0.0075 days to stop the drift of the calendar with respect to the equinox. The equinox is the moment when the visible sun is directly above the equator. This occurs twice a year, in September and in March.

Secondly, in the years since the First Council of Nicaea in AD 325, the excess leap days introduced by the Julian algorithm had caused the calendar to drift such that the spring equinox was occurring well before its nominal 21st of March date. This date was important to the Christian churches because it is fundamental to the calculation of the date of Easter or as some of us Pentecostals would say, Resurrection Sunday. To reinstate the association, the reform advanced the date by 10 days: Thursday 4 October 1582 was followed by Friday 15 October 1582. They skipped 14 days to adapt to the new calendar.

The reform was adopted initially by the Catholic countries of Europe and their overseas possessions. Over the next three centuries, the Protestant and Eastern Orthodox countries also moved to what they called the *Improved calendar*, with Greece being the last European country to adopt the calendar (for civil use only) in 1923.

Just like the Julian calendar proposed by Julius Caesar in 708, the Gregorian calendar year consists of 365 days, 12 months consisting of 28-31 days. A year is the time it takes for the earth to revolve around the sun. A month is the measured time of the movement of the moon. The word month and moon have the same root. A month is the time it takes for the moon to revolve around the earth. Lastly, a day is the time it takes the earth to complete a full turn on its axis.

The names of the months are all significant in Roman culture. The months have been named after gods and emperors.

January is named after the Roman god Janus. He had two faces so he could see the future and the past! He was also the god of doors.

February is named after the ancient roman festival of purification called Februa.

March is named after Mars, the roman god of war.

April takes its name from the Latin word *aperire*, meaning, "to open" (*as flowers do in spring*)

May is named after the Greek goddess Maia.

June is named after the Roman goddess Juno – the god of marriage and childbirth.

July is named after Julius Caesar, the Roman statesman.

August is named after Rome's first emperor Augustus.

September, October, November, and December are named after Roman numbers 7, 8, 9 and 10. They were originally the seventh, eighth, ninth and tenth months of the Roman year.

THE NEED TO PROPHESY DAILY

Blessed be the Lord, who daily loadeth us with benefits, even the
God of our salvation. Selah. *Psalms 68:19*

Now that we have explored the origin and significance of numbers
and we have examined the calendar and its origin, I want to share
with you the importance of daily prophecy. In order to do this, we
must take a look at what prophecy really is.

In its simplest form, prophecy is the foretelling and forth telling of
the mind and heart of God. To foretell is to predict or forecast the
future. Prophecy comes to tell us what will happen next and what
lies ahead. It is a grave mistake to believe that prophecy comes to
only confirm, because we all do not know the future or what is in
front of us. But prophecy can reveal what is unknown. Isaiah 7:14
says *"Therefore the Lord himself shall give you a sign; Behold, a virgin
shall conceive, and bear a son, and shall call his name Immanuel."* In
this text the prophet Isaiah is predicting the future that the messiah
is coming. He is foretelling what will happen. Though it was
centuries later that this prophecy manifested, it was still prophecy,
nonetheless.

Prophecy is also forth telling. It not only foresees the future, but
prophecy can create the future. In 2 Kings 4:16 *"And he said, About
this season, according to the time of life, thou shalt embrace a son. And she
said, Nay, my lord, thou man of God, do not lie unto thine handmaid."*
Elisha speaks to the Shunemite woman and he creates a future for
her because of her kindness to him. She was not supposed to have
a child, but the prophet created the future through the prophetic
word.

Prophecy is the Word of the Lord revealed to humanity. It is what is on the mind of God, and it is publicized through prophets and those who have the gift of prophecy.

One might ask, well then why would we need prophecy daily? There are several reasons given to us in scripture that the word of God should be an everyday desire. It was taught to us by Jesus in the model prayer in Matthew 6:11 *"Give us this day our daily bread."* Here Jesus trained the disciples to demand of God a daily portion from heaven. This was not a request for bread; it was a demand for bread. He said Give us... Then Jesus himself said in John 6:48 *"I am that bread of life."* Jesus himself is the bread of life that He told us to demand of the Father to give. This notes that daily we are to demand of God a deposit of Jesus.

Furthermore, Jesus is the living Word! John 1:1 states "In the beginning was the Word, and the Word was with God, and the Word was God." So daily we need a living word that gives us life. A word that will foretell what lies ahead A word that will create a future that will not exist except this word is given. We need prophecy daily.

In Psalm 68 verse 19 it says blessed be the Lord... The word blessed here is *'barak'* which means blessed and filled with strength or lightning. The word lord is the word *'ani'* which means *"I am here"*

It then says that He daily loads us with benefits... The word loadeth here means to load with a burden. Not all burdens are bad. In Matthew 11:30 Jesus states *'For my yoke is easy, and my burden is light.'* So, when God burdens us with something it simply means He is overwhelming us with a thing, more than we have ever had or possessed before. Then the word benefit is the word 'gemul', which means to reward or what is deserved.

This text, in its original language tells us that the Lord who is filled with strength is present with us and He burdens us with rewards that we deserve. Then it says even the God of our salvation. Salvation here is deliverance and victory. So, what is deserved is merciful in that it is not according to our sin, it is in accordance with our victory in deliverance. This is what God wants us to have daily. He wants us loaded down with victory and deliverance every single day.

Lastly, the word 'selah' that we often see in the Psalms is a behavior to be demonstrated more than a word to be read. Because the Psalms are songs that are to be sung before the Lord, there were times when the musicians would simply play the instruments and the people would think about the lyrics they just sang. A Selah moment is a moment of meditation and deep thought about the lyrics previously rendered. God wants us to not only be loaded down with benefits, but He also desires that we mediate and think about them as we celebrate His wondrous works.

It is my hope and prayer that you would receive every word of prophecy everyday that is written in this book. The heart and the mind of God is being revealed to you through numbers and dates. God prophesies to you daily what will be and what to expect. Allow the daily prophecy to speak to you and over your day. Allow it to create the future you desire and warn you of what is up the road.

I have prayed and sought the Lord for each day of prophecy. I have heard from Him, and He has spoken to me concerning you. Each day is filled with Gods thoughts about you. Particularly your birthday is a date that you might be most interested in seeing and hear the word of the Lord for you on the date of the celebration of your birth. Receive the word of the Lord for your birthday.

JANUARY

"The Month of God"

JANUARY 1

Today God places Himself before you. He is in front of your day and in front of your year. Today you will see the Lord God before you. You will know what it means to have Him before you in the beginning of everything you do and will accomplish this year. This is your God Day! As God remains first in your life and all you do, you will see His fullness manifested completely. You will not fail because God is first!

I prophesy that nothing will be impossible to you because God is with you. All that God has determined for you will come to pass. God is ever before you and in front. If you keep Him first and ultimate, no good thing will be kept from you. The Lord God opens to you opportunity and breaks down the oppositions that hinders you today and this year. Today is your God Day!

Isaiah 45:2 - I will go before thee, and make the crooked places straight: I will break in pieces the gates of brass, and cut in sunder the bars of iron:

JANUARY 2

Today you will witness God and His Glory! You will see second hand the handiwork of God. You will hear the good news of the future He has prepared and planned for you. You will walk in the steps of His will. God will show you what is to come, and you will know it. You will be a witness to the power of God today.

I prophesy that you will testify to others what God has done for you. You will spread the good news of His blessings and favor upon you. Today you carry the grace to be a witness of who God is. Many will come to know Him through your testimony and your witness. Your life testifies that God exist and is very real. God uses your life and experiences to testify of His power.

Exodus 14:13 - And Moses said unto the people, Fear ye not, stand still, and see the salvation of the Lord, which he will shew to you today: for the Egyptians whom ye have seen to day, ye shall see them again no more for ever.

JANUARY 3

Today is the day that you experience Gods divinity! You will know Him in His fullness and the manifestation of His Glory. God's desire for you is that you will know Him in every way. Today He introduces Himself to you in new ways and new dimensions.

I prophesy that you will know Him as Father and provider. You will receive the comfort and identity that only He can give. Today you will know Him as Son and Savior. You will receive the inheritance of sonship and possess the confidence of His redeeming quality. Today you will understand the power of the Holy Spirit that dwells within you. He will lead and guide you. Today the complete Godhead stands with you!

1 John 5:8 - And there are three that bear witness in earth, the Spirit, and the water, and the blood: and these three agree in one.

JANUARY 4

Today the winds of God blow in your direction! Everything that was stagnant and stuck begins to move again with the wind of God. Gods wind causes hindrances and debris to blow away from your life. Today God sends winds from the East, West, North and South to blow and causes you to move into new areas and territory.

I prophesy that you will flow with God's wind today. It may be different and unfamiliar, but may you discern that it is God that is blowing. He causes the winds from heaven to blow the blessing into your life. New things are coming your way and the winds of God will deliver them to you.

Genesis 8:1 - And God remembered Noah, and every living thing, and all the cattle that was with him in the ark: and God made a wind to pass over the earth, and the waters asswaged.

JANUARY 5

Today you will experience God's Grace and Favor! The favor of God follows you everywhere you go and everything that you do. Things that were a struggle to accomplish will now come easy due to the favor of God that is upon you and with you. God's favor surrounds you completely. There is no area of your life untouched by His Grace. Today God's favor protects you from adversarial attacks. It surrounds you completely. Your home, family, life, and possessions are all covered in this favor.

I prophesy that you live in this supernatural realm of God's favor. May you experience the things that heaven promised you. Favor is your flavor; it is your fragrance and your future. Today you obtain favor with God! It is because of this favor that is upon you that you will have uncommon support, blessings, and benefits. This is not mans faor, but God's favor. Receive it!

Psalms 5:12 - For thou, Lord, wilt bless the righteous; with favour wilt thou compass him as with a shield.

JANUARY 6

Today you partner with God to accomplish your purpose in the earth. The Lord God has plans for you that are good and not bad. May you come into complete agreement with God concerning who you are and what you are called to do. Today you will experience the amazing infusion of man in complete agreement with God; earth and heaven working in conjunction with each other on your behalf. Humanity and divinity in perfect partnership is the order of the day.

I prophesy to your body, soul, and spirit that they all come into full alignment with what God is doing within you today. As you put God first, you will see the benefits of His leading and guiding you into the right path and making the right decisions.

Matthew 6:10 - Thy kingdom come. Thy will be done in earth, as it is in heaven.

JANUARY 7

Today God makes everything complete in your life. The Lord God causes you to be full and perfect (mature). Everything that is meant for you and your life of godliness is provided. You have all that you need. God makes it complete today. There is no need to look further for the tools for your future. The Lord God has placed them within you. You have been perfectly designed, equipped, and supplied with all that is needed for you to fulfill your purpose in God.

I prophesy that you walk in an assurance today that all that is needed has been supplied. God is complete and He has made you complete and perfect. God's ability to finish everything He starts is expressed through you today. You are not incomplete, you are not fragmented, you are not in pieces. You are completely whole. You are completely healed. You are completely restored. You are completely blessed. For the hand of Lord God has done this unto you.

Philippians 1:6 - Being confident of this very thing, that he which hath begun a good work in you will perform it until the day of Jesus Christ:

JANUARY 8

Today God relates with you in a new way! The old you will give way to the new. Your attitude, perception, and mindset, all operate in a new place. God provokes you to experience the New that He has to offer. You will experience God in a new way. You will see and hear from Him in ways that you have never done so before. Your relationship with God goes to new realms. He has wanted to speak to you and minister to you in ways that were previously hindered. But today as the sun rose, so did the new things that God desires to show you.

I prophesy that your eyes be open to see God in a new way. May your ears be open to hear from God in a new way. May your feet be prepared to walk with God in a new way. May your hands be lifted to surrender to God in a new way. May your heart be open to God in a new way. May your mouth speak to God in a new way. May your spirit yield to God in a new way.

Isaiah 43:19 - Behold, I will do a new thing; now it shall spring forth; shall ye not know it? I will even make a way in the wilderness, and rivers in the desert.

JANUARY 9

Today you experience God's deliverance. You will breakthrough to understand Gods fullness. Today is the day you experience a release of all the hindrances that has limited the god encounters of your life. The Lord has been desiring to show you Himself in new ways and in new dimensions. Today is the day that the will of God is fulfilled in your life. This is God's deliverance for you. This is God's breakthrough for you.

I prophesy that the walls of hindrances come down in front of you. The sea of stagnation opens before you and permits you to walk into your promised victory of God's presence. You have been limited and held back far too long. Breakthrough today and experience God in His fullness.

Psalms 56:13 - For thou hast delivered my soul from death: wilt not thou deliver my feet from falling, that I may walk before God in the light of the living?

JANUARY 10

Today God brings your life into order. Chaos gives way to organization and the law of order. Your life comes into godly alignment of order today. Every law that dictates your life is influenced and impacted by Elohim. Disorder and disorganization are no more for you. You have been assessed and tried concerning promotion and progress. Today you are rewarded with them because proper order has had its perfect way.

I prophesy that you accept the grace to be organized and disciplined in your life. God gives you the ability to manage, maintain and mature every excellent work. It is God that gives you the power to get wealth and today your discipline will reward you with clarity.

1 Corinthians 14:40 - Let all things be done decently and in order.

JANUARY 11

Today God graces you to complete all the tasks that have been lingering and are incomplete in your life. You are given the opportunity to finish the tasks you have been given. Time is your ally today. The Joy of the Lord is your strength. Strength is your companion and completion is your goal. Everything you have set as a goal shall be accomplished. You will leave nothing open or undone. You have the grace to finish it.

I prophesy today that all distractions and hindrances are rebuked that cause you to leave tasks and assignments incomplete. God removes blockages from the pipeline of your success. Goals will be met, and purpose will be fulfilled.

Philippians 1:6 - Being confident of this very thing, that he which hath begun a good work in you will perform it until the day of Jesus Christ:

JANUARY 12

Today God's order and government prevails in your life. Today you walk in apostolic fulfillment. God releases His order in your life. That which was promised and prophesied comes into divine order. The government of heaven comes to the earth, and you are the recipient of its benefits. Angels and the heavenly host bring your life into alignment with the order of heaven.

Today I prophesy that your life reflects what is determined in heaven by God almighty. Today you yield your members, your dreams, your ambitions, and your life into divine order. God's order prevails above all other rules and orders. Heavenly order manifests for you today.

Matthew 6:10 - Thy kingdom come. Thy will be done in earth, as it is in heaven

JANUARY 13

Today God releases the double portion in your life. The double portion of God is now touching that which was bare, lacking, or void due to rebellion or disobedience. God fills your cup with double provision. Waywardness has had its work in your life, but this day it gives way to the divine portion of God. God's provision brings your life back into perfect peace and favor.

I prophesy to your heart that you choose to resist the plans of rebellion and disobedience that you may see the fullness of God in your life. May you break the tie with the tings that are contrary to God's will for your life. All soul ties, all contrary relationships and all diabolical activities are rebuked that you might experience God's double portion for you today.

Genesis 48:22 - Moreover I have given to thee one portion above thy brethren, which I took out of the hand of the Amorite with my sword and with my bow.

JANUARY 14

Today God's grace and favor visits you. The judgment and trials that are experienced by others, passes over you. Because of your sacrifices, God causes His wrath and vengeance to pass over you and you will not see it in your house. God saves you from the enemies of your future. Today your enemies will not find your house and you will walk in the victorious testimony of safety.

I prophesy that God keeps your home, your marriage, your children, your businesses, and all that pertains to you safe. He shall defend you, protect you and cover you. God keeps you in the city, the country, when you come in and when you go out. Nothing by any means shall hurt or harm you.

Exodus 12:23 - For the Lord will pass through to smite the Egyptians; and when he seeth the blood upon the lintel, and on the two side posts, the Lord will pass over the door, and will not suffer the destroyer to come in unto your houses to smite you.

JANUARY 15

Today you receive God's Rest! The toiling of your life and all your responsibilities has overwhelmed you. But the Lord will give you rest. Rest in knowing that the Lord God is with you everywhere you go. Rest in the assurance that He will protect you from all hurt and harm. If challenges arise today, they will be met with the presence of God, and you will rest in knowing that all is well.

Today I prophetically speak to your mind, body, and spirit that they all receive divine rest. This rest is not just mere relaxation, but it is an inner knowing that all will be well. This rest brings you energy and strength to allow you to meet every assignment with full presence. Today you show up rested!

Isaiah 30:15 - For thus saith the Lord God, the Holy One of Israel; In returning and rest shall ye be saved; in quietness and in confidence shall be your strength: and ye would not.

JANUARY 16

Today God's Love fills you, surrounds you and satisfies the longing of your soul. You will experience the Love of God in new ways that establishes you and secures you. May you be overwhelmed by the Love of God in ways that causes you to share and express that love with others. God says to you today that He Loves you with an everlasting Love. His love never fails and will never fade away. Despite all that has occurred in your life, God says He loves you still.

I prophesy the Love of God into your life. I prophesy that you will walk in that Love for the rest of your days and that you will never be ashamed of it. I speak into your spirit a confidence that comes from the Love of God. You are Loved by the greatest. You are Loved by Love; You are Loved by God.

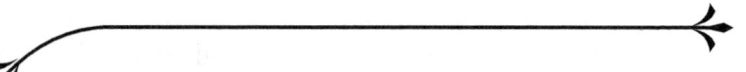

1 John 4:8 - He that loveth not knoweth not God;
for God is love.

JANUARY 17

Today you walk with God! This is the day that you see your life in perfect alignment with the will of God, the purpose of God and the plan of God. You will witness perfect alignment with God. All things that are out of the order of God for your life comes perfectly together. Your life aligns with God. That which was in disarray or discombobulated pulls itself in order due to your alignment with God.

I prophesy that as you align with God so does your life line up with God's will. Today is the day where your YES meets God's AMEN!

Genesis 5:24 - And Enoch walked with God: and he was not; for God took him.

JANUARY 18

Today God binds you to LIFE! All death is rebuked and backed up. God breathes life and new life into you. The enemy comes to kill but Jesus causes you to live. You are so bound to live that all that causes you to die, dies. Live in God. Live in Peace. Live in Love. Live in Joy. Live!

I prophesy life into you today in every area that concerns you. Life to your spirit, life to your mind and life to your body. I speak to your body that years are added to your days. I speak to your spirit that the Spirit of God quickens it, and eternal life is the result. I prophesy to your heart and soul that you see life in its fullness, and you behold all that life has to offer you.

Psalms 118:17 - I shall not die, but live, and declare the works of the Lord.

JANUARY 19

Today God decides on matters that have been taunting you. Today God brings finality to all that has been left open and undecided. God's judgment is released upon those who wish to do you harm and hurt you. The matters of uncertainty and that which is unclear, God makes the final decision today. DO not mourn or weep over the decision of God. He knows what is best and His judgments are final.

I prophesy that you can manage the choices that God makes even those that you do not agree with. I prophesy that you trust in God totally and completely with His decisions.

Psalms 35:24 - Judge me, O Lord my God, according to thy righteousness; and let them not rejoice over me.

JANUARY 20

Today God completes a cycle in your life. As you experience changes and evolution, you begin to fulfill every level completely. God takes you to new levels and experience new dimensions of living, ministry, and business. All the vicious cycles of hindrances and violations are ending today. Every trigger of the past that torments your mind and heart is over today.

I prophesy that you are walking into a new level of wholeness and completion. The tours of the past are ending, and you are about to embark upon fresh territory and terrain. I speak prophetically that you will redeem the time and the years that you wasted. God will restore and bring you into victory.

Colossians 2:10 - And ye are complete in him, which is the head of all principality and power:

JANUARY 21

Today God breaks the will within you to operate in anything that does not please Him. Release the willingness to sabotage what has already been declared over you. Your future was determined before you were born. You must come to agreement with it in all your ways. Refuse to covenant with anything or anyone that will take you out of the will of God.

I prophesy that you walk in new avenues of wisdom and discipline that will provoke conviction in you to obey the purpose of God over your life. I prophetically declare that you yield to the law of God within you. I speak life to your obedience that brings you a harvest of life and peace.

Romans 8:13 - For if ye live after the flesh, ye shall die: but if ye through the Spirit do mortify the deeds of the body, ye shall live.

JANUARY 22

Today God makes you happy! Happiness is the will of God concerning you. Your smile is on the agenda of God. The things that have hovered over your life that cause grief and sorrow are no more. God causes heaven to be on assignment towards you. Sadness breaks today. Pain breaks today. Bitterness breaks today. God overwhelms you with His presence, which brings about a peace and tranquility and it births new laughter within you.

I prophesy to you that you will experience happiness from God that overtakes your soul. There is now an inner joy that soothes and calms your doubts and fears. I prophesy that you are a happy person. I speak the brightness of Gods glory light to shine through you.

Psalms 144:15 - Happy is that people, that is in such a case: yea, happy is that people, whose God is the Lord.

JANUARY 23

Today God causes you to produce productivity. There shall be perpetual productivity coming from you. What you produce will also produce. God gives you residual wealth, residual vision, and residual harvests. There will never be a dry season in your life. It is God that makes this happen for you. It is His continual power of productivity that causes you to do the same.

I prophesy that you produce like God does. I prophesy that there will be generations still reaping the harvest of the decisions you make today. You will have a legacy of production and multiple harvests. Your wells will never dry, your barn will never be empty, and your storehouse will always be full.

2 Corinthians 9:11 - Being enriched in every thing to all bountifulness, which causeth through us thanksgiving to God.

JANUARY 24

Today God uses you as priest! As you make sacrifices for others, the Lord God will respond to every sacrifice with grace and favor. As priest, today is the day that your prayers are heard in heaven. As you petition the Lord, He is ready to hear and answer you today. Every sacrifice and prayer you make and submit to the Lord for others, God will answer. Jesus Christ, your High Priest works a work in you that will show forth His praise and glory. Today you will know the Lord Jesus as your priest.

I prophetically speak that not only will you serve as priest for others, but also today you make sacrifices for yourself. Forgiveness, reconciliation, and atonement with God are all yours today. Your eyes will behold the great harvest of your future as you go before God, and He reveals Himself to you in a glorious way.

1 Peter 2:9 - But ye are a chosen generation, a royal priesthood, an holy nation, a peculiar people; that ye should show forth the praises of him who hath called you out of darkness into his marvelous light:

#GwendasGod

JANUARY 25

Today God releases to you Grace multiplied. Not only does grace come to you multiplied, but it also comes to you in multiple areas. God is the giver of grace, and He gives it to you freely. God's grace causes favor to come to your business endeavors. God's multiplied grace comes to prosper you in your business above that which you have imagined. This is the day you will see it with your own eyes.

I prophesy to you that the grace of God extended to you is paying off debt, satisfying bills, healing your body, and enabling you to perform in ways that you have never operated in before. I prophesy that the multiplied grace of God upon you stretches you to new levels of function and behaviors.

Psalms 84:11 - For the Lord God is a sun and shield: the Lord will give grace and glory: no good thing will he withhold from them that walk uprightly.

JANUARY 26

Today you will see God in numerous ways. Look for Him to show up in different forms and ways in your life. He will not come to you in the ways He has before. But He desires to show you new parts of Him that you have never seen before. You will see God in difficult areas, and you will see God in small areas. Open your eyes today, you will see God show Himself mighty and strong on your behalf.

I prophesy that you will not walk in blindness to the sightings of the Lord God. Your eyes are sharpened, and your discernment is heightened to behold the Lord. You will not miss God today. The image of His presence will be pervasive and clear to you.

Colossians 1:15 - Who is the image of the invisible God, the firstborn of every creature:

JANUARY 27

Today you will experience God's saving power. Salvation comes to your house today. God touches the heart of you and your loved ones, and you will see your family yield to the power of God. Salvation comes to you in ways that cause you to escape terror. God provides salvation to you through Jesus Christ, and you will reap the full benefits of His sacrifice.

I prophesy that the power of salvation is full and evident with you. I prophesy that you will not behold danger or turmoil. You will only see the reward of the faithful. Today God saves you from attacks and persecutions. It will not come near you.

Psalms 118:25 - Save now, I beseech thee, O Lord: O Lord, I beseech thee, send now prosperity.

JANUARY 28

Today God perfects that which concerns you. God causes you to experience perfection in the earth. Exactly what you need and when you need it will be available for you. The right scenario is being prepared for your arrival. You will meet the right person who will provide opportunity to the next area of your life. Things will be perfect for you in so many ways.

I prophesy to you today that you walk perfectly before the Lord. I prophesy that your feet carry you to the perfect place at the perfect time to meet the perfect person. I prophesy that it all aligns perfectly with what God has ordained for you.

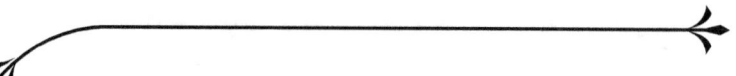

Psalms 138:8 - The Lord will perfect that which concerneth me: thy mercy, O Lord, endureth for ever: forsake not the works of thine own hands.

JANUARY 29

Today embrace change. God comes to change you into better. Do not avoid or resist change. It will work for you and in ways that you need for your future. God provokes change because He knows what is ahead. As you adapt to new things and evolve into a new you, you will begin to see the reason for the change. God is changing things around you by changing you.

I prophesy that you will yield to the new you that is evolving. I prophesy that you approach this new season with boldness and confidence. You will not live in fear or lack clarity. I send God's winds of change towards you that will blow you into new realms and new dimensions.

Hebrews 7:12 - For the priesthood being changed, there is made of necessity a change also of the law.

JANUARY 30

Today God sets you a part for a magnificent work in the Kingdom. You must consecrate yourself today. The Lord God is calling you higher to another place in Him. This level of consecration will reveal the complete will of God concerning you and what He has called you to do. As you submit to this lifestyle of consecration, you will begin to be used of the Lord in new ways and understand the mysteries of God.

I prophesy that today is the day that you walk in maturity for ministry and the call of God on your life. Your mind is renewed, and your heart is fixed to serve the Lord Christ and with a perfect heart you say YES to Him! As you matriculate in the Lord your yes will become stronger and your willingness to serve Him will be strengthened.

1 Chronicles 29:5 - The gold for things of gold, and the silver for things of silver, and for all manner of work to be made by the hands of artificers. And who then is willing to consecrate his service this day unto the Lord?

JANUARY 31

Today you will know another name of God. God has shown you Himself in many ways, but today you will know another form of God. Today God glorifies Himself through you. His name will go throughout the earth as you arrive victoriously to the end of every trial. God writes His name in your heart that you may know Him more and be called by His name.

I prophesy to you today that you name the name of God in all that you do. I speak that you will not be ashamed of His name and your boldness will release victories in your life. I speak over your heart that you will love the name of God. I speak over your mind that you will think always on Him. I speak over your endeavors that His name will ring out and the multitude will be drawn to you because of it.

Proverbs 18:10 - The name of the Lord is a strong tower: the righteous runneth into it, and is safe.

FEBRUARY

"The Month of Witness"

FEBRUARY 1

Today is the day that you will witness God. You will see God in ways you have never seen Him before. Your eyes will behold His majesty. Your ears will hear His voice. Your heart will witness His love. Your hand will hold His provisions. Your feet will walk in His ways and your mind will be full of Him.

I prophesy that as you witness the work of God in your life, you will begin to trust Him more. I prophesy that you will observe all the good pleasures He has in store for you, and you will rejoice and be glad. Today you will witness God... expect it!

1 John 5:9 - If we receive the witness of men, the witness of God is greater: for this is the witness of God which he hath testified of his Son.

FEBRUARY 2

Today God brings into your life new partnerships. These partnerships will testify to your skills and abilities. The Lord compliments all that He has placed upon your life with conglomerates that will glorify Him. You will not have to work alone. You will not have to go alone. The Lord sends you gifts that will walk and work with you.

I prophesy to you today that your heart will be healed to welcome the new partners into your life. As you witness new relationships, may you be open to receive and cooperate with your restoration. Open your eyes, you will see it!

Acts 14:17 - Nevertheless he left not himself without witness, in that he did good, and gave us rain from heaven, and fruitful seasons, filling our hearts with food and gladness.

FEBRUARY 3

Today you will witness God's fullness in your life. The Lord God desires to express His complete divinity to you. He will hold no good thing from you. You will know Him as Father who provides and protects you. You will know Him as Savior and redeemer who paid the price for your eternal salvation. You will know Him as Holy Spirit who comforts and teaches you all that you need to know. God's complete trinity manifests before you today.

I prophesy that as God reveals Himself to you, that you will be drawn closer to Him. May you be attracted again to Him and desire Him completely. I speak to every hindrance that keeps you separate from Him that it will not prevail. The Father, The Son and The Holy Spirit is within you today. Welcome Him!

1 John 5:7 - For there are three that bear record in heaven, the Father, the Word, and the Holy Ghost: and these three are one.

FEBRUARY 4

Today you will witness the winds blowing your way. God causes the four winds of the earth to blow towards you today. The winds blow in favor and blow out fear. The wind of the earth causes you to walk into unfamiliar places and see new things. You will testify to the blessings of the Lord that is now upon your life. You will be a witness of God's supernatural favor.

I prophesy to you today that a mighty rushing wind comes to accelerate you to another place in your life. This wind pushes you into fresh territory and strengthens you to be bold and courageous. I speak blessings, favor, and provision to come from the north, south, east, and west. From all directions you will see the goodness of the Lord. Each time you turn there will be blessings.

Genesis 28:14 - And thy seed shall be as the dust of the earth, and thou shalt spread abroad to the west, and to the east, and to the north, and to the south: and in thee and in thy seed shall all the families of the earth be blessed.

FEBRUARY 5

Today you will watch favor work for you! The things that you found challenging or difficult to accomplish, favor will bring to pass with ease. You will be a witness to what happens when favor flows through your life. You will tell others that God has done this, and it is marvelous in our eyes. Where your money is lacking, favor will make up the difference.

I prophesy that God removes the sting of struggle out of your process. I prophesy that you will have sweatless victories that will be miraculous and noteworthy. Be not ashamed to testify to others of the favor. God has decided to grace you and your assignment is to tell others of Hid goodness.

Proverbs 3:4 - So shalt thou find favour and good understanding in the sight of God and man.

FEBRUARY 6

Today you will see God complete you. God is forming you and making you into His own image. The stretching the pulling and the pain you have been experiencing is all due to the formation that God has been doing with you. He is removing all that does not look like Him or pleases Him. He is adding all that will glorify Him. Allow the Lord God to work a work with you. When He is done, you will resemble His son.

I prophesy to you today that you will not resist the work that the Lord is doing with you. I prophesy that you will be patient and receptive to the form He is developing. I speak the breath of God to blow within you, that you are not left void or empty of His presence. As you are fully present with this process you will rejoice in the completion of who you are.

Genesis 1:26 - And God said, Let us make man in our image, after our likeness: and let them have dominion over the fish of the sea, and over the fowl of the air, and over the cattle, and over all the earth, and over every creeping thing that creepeth upon the earth.

FEBRUARY 7

Today you will behold conclusion. God is bringing closure to open chapters of your life. You will see yourself on the other side of things that used to torment you. You will perceive yourself whole and healed from the issues of the past. Things that lingered will be final and end.

I prophesy a benediction over the former things. I speak to your mind and heart that you will be fully complete with the things of old and that you will not return to it. God is finished with that part of your story, now you must be as well.

Exodus 14:13 - And Moses said unto the people, Fear ye not, stand still, and see the salvation of the Lord, which he will shew to you to day: for the Egyptians whom ye have seen to day, ye shall see them again no more for ever.

FEBRUARY 8

Now that a cycle is complete, today you will behold a new chapter in your life. Be prepared to embrace new things. Today you will witness new beginnings. God has prepared you for today and you have all that you need to meet the requirements of the day. Approach today with boldness and refuse to be fearful. The Lord is with you.

I prophesy that you will not be afraid of the changes and the new things that are before you. I speak holy boldness upon you to conquer the assignments that heaven has given you. You are strengthened today to meet it withal.

Isaiah 42:9 - Behold, the former things are come to pass, and new things do I declare: before they spring forth I tell you of them.

FEBRUARY 9

Today is the day to witness a breakthrough. You will break through the walls and ceilings of bondage and hindrances that have held you back. All that you have desired to see and walk into will be made manifest beginning today. For too long you have been stuck and stagnant. But today there is a breakthrough in store for you and you will see it. You will be deputized by heaven as a witness in the earth of breaking through generational curses and oppositional restrictions.

I prophesy to you today that you will see what your patience and endurance has paid off. The reward of your durability will be manifested in coming through to meet your purpose. I prophesy that you are being delivered into a new place of peace and pleasures.

Ecclesiastes 9:11 - I returned, and saw under the sun, that the race is not to the swift, nor the battle to the strong, neither yet bread to the wise, nor yet riches to men of understanding, nor yet favour to men of skill; but time and chance happeneth to them all.

FEBRUARY 10

Today you will witness your authority having weight in the spirit and in the natural. You have been given authority on the earth and you will behold the power of that authority. Things that are given under your care will become subject to you and yield to you the results of your vision. Your rule will not be ignored or overlooked. Your commands will be met with execution.

I prophesy to you today that as you submit yourself to God that things will submit to you. Your authority on the earth increases more and more so that you may begin to walk in your ordain giftings. You will see the manifestation of this beginning today.

Matthew 18:18 - Verily I say unto you,
Whatsoever ye shall bind on earth shall be bound
in heaven: and whatsoever ye shall loose on earth
shall be loosed in heaven.

FEBRUARY 11

Today God will reveal to you who and what has been holding you back. Your future and destiny have been awaiting you but there has been opposition that you have been unaware of. Today God shines a light on the things and the people who have been operating covertly to oppose you. No longer will you be blinded to the stubbornness of people who will not budge. God will show you and you will see it.

I prophesy to you that you walk in such a wisdom that when your eyes see your opposition you will know exactly what to say and do. May you begin to testify of the grace of God with you that He will not leave you ignorant concerning the enemy's devices. All that you need to know is about to be revealed and you will know how to manage it.

2 Corinthians 2:11 - Lest Satan should get an advantage of us: for we are not ignorant of his devices.

FEBRUARY 12

Today you will witness divine order coming into manifestation. All the things you have experienced were for this time and season in your life. God is bringing all things into order as He has ordained it to be so. The things that you have prayed for are all falling into the order of God. The Lord God has ordered your steps and has ordained an end for you. You will meet it withal.

I prophesy to you today that you will see the fullness of God's order for your life. There is a prevailing will of God that will influence your will. The divine will of God will be made manifest for you in every way. Open your eyes today and see what the Lord has ordered for you.

Psalms 37:23 - The steps of a good man are ordered by the Lord: and he delighteth in his way.

FEBRUARY 13

Today God reveals to you your rebelliousness. There are things that God has been showing you and telling you to do. You have often omitted to do them. But His grace causes you to witness it and make new decisions. When the Lord reveals this to you simply repent and move into total obedience. His glory will be revealed within you.

Today I prophesy to you that you embrace radical obedience. I prophesy that your will dies to the will of God concerning you. May you walk in total obedience to what the Lord commands you to do. He loves you with an everlasting love and He will not suffer you to be out of His will. I say that rebellion has no place within you, and you are free from its fruit.

1 Samuel 15:22 - And Samuel said, Hath the Lord as great delight in burnt offerings and sacrifices, as in obeying the voice of the Lord? Behold, to obey is better than sacrifice, and to hearken than the fat of rams.

FEBRUARY 14

Today you will witness the love God towards you through His unfailing Grace. The Lord causes the afflictions that effects others to pass by you today. The harm, the destruction will not find you. Because of your sacrifice, you will see the Lord pass over you with these things. They will not meet you or come to your house. God's love surrounds you to protect you and you will behold it and testify of it.

I prophesy to you today that you will share the love of God to others, and they too will know the unfailing grace of God. What you have been given freely, so do you share with others. May God use you to spread abroad the remarkable things He has done for you.

Lamentations 3:23 - They are new every morning: great is thy faithfulness.

FEBRUARY 15

Open your eyes and mind to what today has to offer you. God will cause you to experience a retreat from your toiling. Today the Lord rebukes burn out and fatigue within you. You will not breakdown from being overwhelmed. May you experience divine restoration of strength and virtue.

I prophesy to you today that you be restored from within. I speak to your body, your soul, and your spirit that each of them receives rejuvenation and revival. It is not the Lords will that you continue in exhaustion. But today the word rest is spoken; hear and receive it.

Exodus 15:27 - And they came to Elim, where were twelve wells of water, and threescore and ten palm trees: and they encamped there by the waters.

FEBRUARY 16

Today you will witness Love. Not only does God love you, but also people also love you. You do not have to seek out this love; it is already there. Love surrounds you. There are those who love you for who you are and not what you do. You will experience this love today. You are also a vessel of love. You are called to share love to others and express to them the love of God and the love you have for them.

I prophesy to you that you be not afraid to receive and express love. May you be free from the past relationships that hurt you that caused you not to love or trust. Let today be the beginning of your new perspective on love and the way you will share it with others.

1 Peter 4:8 - And above all things have fervent charity among yourselves: for charity shall cover the multitude of sins.

FEBRUARY 17

Today you will witness spiritual alignment. Things that you have been praying for and things you have been seeking are all aligning with the will and purpose of God. God causes you to see the grounds moving in your favor. He will not simply move you, but He will move the very ground you stand on to align you with what He desires for you. Get ready to see it.

I prophesy to you today that you settle yourself in the things of God so that you do not miss this next shift for your life. It is a divine movement that is taking place and you need to settle in God to be stable to survive it. Your world is about to change for the better and you will know that it is God.

Romans 8:28 - And we know that all things work together for good to them that love God, to them who are the called according to his purpose.

FEBRUARY 18

Today step out of your comfort zone and live. There is so much life that God desires you to live. You are not limited to one area, one region or one gift. You are called to live an abundant life in Christ. Today God reminds you to live. There are things you must witness and things you must behold. An abundant life is your portion today.

I prophesy to you today that you use your life to show Gods goodness and grace. I speak abundant fervor upon you that you will go out and tell everyone you know and meet about the life Christ has given you. It is an abundant life, it is a God life, and it is an eternal life. Now live it!

John 10:10 - The thief cometh not, but for to steal, and to kill, and to destroy: I am come that they might have life, and that they might have it more abundantly.

FEBRUARY 19

Today you will witness the harvest from your labor. God causes your fruit to yield increase from the toiling you have done. You have produced fruit that will not fade away or be destroyed. Your fruit will remain. You have been waiting for this season to come and now it is here. Behold the season of production. Your fruitfulness is upon you.

I prophesy to you today that God testifies of your labor by causing you to be fruitful. I release supernatural increase upon all your efforts that they experience divine light and glorious moisture. God decides today to release you into increase.

John 15:16 - Ye have not chosen me, but I have chosen you, and ordained you, that ye should go and bring forth fruit, and that your fruit should remain: that whatsoever ye shall ask of the Father in my name, he may give it you.

FEBRUARY 20

Today you will behold the redemption of that which you have lost. God will cause you to redeem the lost time, the lost resources, the lost joy, and lost peace you have experienced. Everything that was taken, lost, or destroyed will be restored back to you. You will see how it all comes back.

I prophesy to you today divine restoration. I speak about every area of your life that experiences the fullness of restoration. Your tears and sorrows have repurchased your possessions. It all returns to you better than before. Get ready to see it.

Joel 2:25 - And I will restore to you the years that the locust hath eaten, the cankerworm, and the caterpiller, and the palmerworm, my great army which I sent among you.

FEBRUARY 21

Today God allows you to witness to the wicked. Today is a day that God desires to use you. His desire is to get the glory out of your life and to save others alive. This will be dome as you go forth as a willing vessel to testify to others of His power to save and deliver. As you share what the Lord has done for you, others will hear of it and desire to have a relationship with Him as well. Lost souls are waiting to hear your testimony.

I prophesy to you today that you go with holy boldness and begin to share your story with others and there will be a great harvest of souls because of your obedience. As you consent to this assignment, rewards and blessings will be upon you and with you for the rest of your days and the world without end.

Acts 1:8 - But ye shall receive power, after that the Holy Ghost is come upon you: and ye shall be witnesses unto me both in Jerusalem, and in all Judaea, and in Samaria, and unto the uttermost part of the earth.

FEBRUARY 22

Today you will see the light of God's glory. Today you walk in glory light. The glory light of God surrounds you and gives you warmth and peace. The glory light of God causes you to walk in a lit path and not be in darkness. You will know what is before you and what is around you. This light will not blind you, but this light will illuminate in such a way to cause you to see well.

I prophesy to you that you posses a glow likened unto Moses when he descended from the mountain due to this light. The brightness of it will be within you that others will see it and glorify your Father. This light is the brightness of His presence.

Matthew 5:16 - Let your light so shine before men, that they may see your good works, and glorify your Father which is in heaven.

FEBRUARY 23

Today you will bring forth the things within you that you have carried. It is now time to deliver. There are great visions that have matriculated in your spirit and God has brought you full circle to deliver them. Prepare yourself to bring forth everything that this season demands. There are those awaiting the arrival of the vision the God gave you.

I prophesy to you that you will be strong to deliver this seed and you will witness what God has placed inside you. You will behold the purpose of your last season and you will count it all joy. Get ready to see what you have been carrying.

Isaiah 66:7 - Before she travailed, she brought forth; before her pain came, she was delivered of a man child.

FEBRUARY 24

Today you will witness God using you to affect the lives of others in a new way. You will be shocked as to how the Lord begins to use you. As you open your mouth, He will speak for you. As you are willing to go, He will lead you. Prepare to see God get the glory out of you through your willingness to be used of Him.

Today I prophesy that your life be a beacon of light that will lead others to Christ. As you witness to them, they will witness the love of God. You then will witness how the Lord has anointed you for now. I speak over your life that you will be a yielded vessel unto honor and glory.

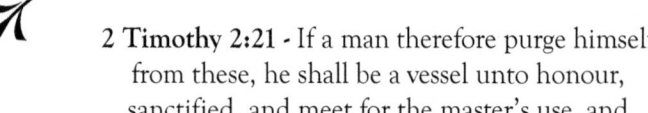

2 Timothy 2:21 - If a man therefore purge himself from these, he shall be a vessel unto honour, sanctified, and meet for the master's use, and prepared unto every good work.

FEBRUARY 25

Today you will see the grace of God overwhelm you and overtake you. Every area of your life will behold the supernatural favor of God. God decides to favor you and there is nothing that can stop it. However, this favor is uncommon in that it overshadows all that you do in every way. The grace God will overtake you; be sure to tell others that the blessing is from above.

I prophesy to you that God greets you each hour of the day with new blessings, new provisions, and more good news. I speak over your finances, your family, and your future that they are all affected by the grace of God, and it becomes so breathtaking that you can't keep it to yourself. Get ready for supernatural grace.

Acts 20:32 - And now, brethren, I commend you
to God, and to the word of his grace, which is able
to build you up, and to give you an inheritance
among all them, which are sanctified.

FEBRUARY 26

Today you will see everything that compliments you for purpose. God will show you His reflection in human form. You will partner with people who have passions, desires and goals like yourself. You will see God form people for you and make them in front of your very eyes.

I prophesy to you today that you begin to embrace the god-sent people designed for your future. I speak a heavy discernment upon you that you can determine who and what is for you. You will know it because it will look like the God within you.

Nehemiah 2:7-8 - Moreover I said unto the king, If it please the king, let letters be given me to the governors beyond the river, that they may convey me over till I come into Judah; And a letter unto Asaph the keeper of the king's forest, that he may give me timber to make beams for the gates of the palace which appertained to the house, and for the wall of the city, and for the house that I shall enter into. And the king granted me, according to the good hand of my God upon me.

FEBRUARY 27

Today you will witness your prayers being answered to save your family. God begins to move in the hearts of your loves ones to save their souls. Salvation comes to your house today. Your family name has reached the heavens and God responds with salvation. Generational curses of waywardness are broken today, and the redeeming quality of God comes to you.

I prophesy that unsaved loved ones will begin to contact you to inquire about your faith, your God, and your church. I declare that the curse of the lost is broken over your family NOW is Jesus' Name! As you behold them giving their life to the Lord, you must rejoice and testify that the Lord has done this thing.

Acts 16:31 - And they said, Believe on the Lord Jesus Christ, and thou shalt be saved, and thy house.

FEBRUARY 28

Today you will embrace fulfillment. You will walk in a place of closure due to tasks and seasons fulfilled. Your eyes will behold the settling of your life due to the season finished and complete. Not only is it over, but it is dome with precision and excellently. You will see the rewards of your potential.

I prophesy to you today that you no longer doubt yourself. But you walk in confidence because you have the potential to complete every assignment successfully. Tasks will not overwhelm you but be met with precision and accuracy in accomplishing them. Rise up today and go forth. Your reward is great.

1 Kings 9:1-2 - And it came to pass, when Solomon had finished the building of the house of the Lord, and the king's house, and all Solomon's desire which he was pleased to do, That the Lord appeared to Solomon the second time, as he had appeared unto him at Gibeon.

FEBRUARY 29

Today you will see change. Change has been searching for you... awaiting you. Change has finally found you and will befriend you. You will see yourself endure changes and embark upon new changes. You are changing for the better. Things will not remain the same because you are different. People around you are changing. Do not blame them; this change is necessary for your destiny and your future.

I prophesy to you today that you begin to evolve into the greatness that you are and that has always been in you. I speak over your life the newness of you. God sends help from His sanctuary to assist you in navigating the new environments that will welcome you. This change is for your good. Embrace it!

1 Samuel 10:6 - And the Spirit of the Lord will come upon thee, and thou shalt prophesy with them, and shalt be turned into another man.

MARCH

"The Month of The Trinity"

MARCH 1

Today the fullness of God surrounds you and satisfies you. Today you walk with God in a new way to embrace all that He must show you and tell you. There are mysteries that God will reveal to you that only He can. His desire is for you to behold His full deity and embrace who He is totally to you. You cannot miss any of Him, for He will come to you in many forms, but it will all be Him.

I prophesy to you today that your discernment is sharpened and your ability to see God even in challenges is heightened. I speak to your eyes and heart that they match and equate in perception. God will show Himself to you and you will not miss Him. Prepare to be protected. Prepare to be saved. Prepare to be filled. God will visit you.

Job 10:12 - Thou hast granted me life and favour, and thy visitation hath preserved my spirit.

MARCH 2

Today all of heaven testifies of you. Your name has been mentioned in the heavenlies and now that sound reverberates in the earth. What God has said about you will be heard here on earth. The world will know what the mind of God is concerning you. We all will hear and know what God has already determined about you. Heaven and the host carry the word of you to the areas of the earth that you will impact.

I prophesy that you fully receive the word of the Lord concerning you. There can be no doubt or fear concerning it. I speak over your heart that it be fixed to fully embrace all that God has said about you. Receive all of it today!

Jeremiah 29:11 - For I know the thoughts that I think toward you, saith the Lord, thoughts of peace, and not of evil, to give you an expected end.

MARCH 3

Today God in His deity brings another dimension of glory to you. There is another height in the spirit that God desires you to arrive to. Today is the day to reach new heights. There is more, there is greater, there is a higher place, and it is calling for you. God desires you to reach for it and obtain it.

Today I prophesy to you that you will no longer settle for mediocrity or low-level living. You are called to higher, and you must get there. I speak to your reach and command it to stretch beyond your perceived limitations. Your faith must stretch today as you achieve a greater grace from God to go up.

Psalms 61:2 - From the end of the earth will I cry unto thee, when my heart is overwhelmed: lead me to the rock that is higher than I.

MARCH 4

Today God is in the wind. You will behold the gusting of God pushing you into purpose. He sends the wind to move you into what He ordained for you. God sends the wind to blow you forward. March forth says the Lord to you today. His winds from all directions will carry you into the right pathway. The winds obey the voice of the Lord, and He has commanded them to transport you. Go with the wind of God today.

I prophesy to you today that fear does not grip your heart. Stagnation does not become your norm. I speak to your feet and will that they both have agility and mobility. May you become unglued from the issues of your past and what holds you back.

Philippians 3:14 - I press toward the mark for the prize of the high calling of God in Christ Jesus.

MARCH 5

Today the fullness of God graces you to accomplish difficult tasks. That which was arduous, that which was challenging, will be no more. The impossible will be possible today. What seemed like would never happen, will be done by miracle or by provision. All of God will ensure that you struggle no more as His grace enables you to do it.

I prophesy to you today that you walk in a new grace of easy labor and quick results. The intensity of bureaucratic systems gives way to the grace of God that is upon you and within you. The red tape of progress yields to God concerning you. You will have supernatural favor for what you need in this season.

Romans 8:31 - What shall we then say to these things? If God be for us, who can be against us?

MARCH 6

Today all of God impacts all of you. Today you stand in the security that you are made in the image and likeness of God. The Father, The Son & The Holy Spirit all influence your Body, your soul, and your spirit. The image of God is reflective in your image, and you will begin to walk in the authority of His image. Begin to accept that you are His on the earth and He is with you.

I prophesy to every part of your existence that you show the image of God wherever you go. When people see you, they will see God in the earth. You carry the name of His son within your head, and you are filled with His Spirit in your soul. Walk boldly with the assurance that God is with you, and you are His.

Colossians 2:9 - For in him the whole fullness of deity dwells bodily,

MARCH 7

The Father, Son, and Holy Spirit, all bring you into maturity. As God is complete and full, so will you be. Everything concerning you matures to a place of performance. You are now ready to move on to what you have been sent to do. Everyone will know who you are in fullness. God completes the process of maturation with you.

I prophesy to you today that you shed the past and get rid of the old. The new things of maturity are now with you. Your money matures. Your mind matures. Your prayer life matures. All to the glory of God! This maturity comes at the time of your life when God is ready to launch you forward. Do not forsake it. Embrace it.

James 2:22 - Seest thou how faith wrought with his works, and by works was faith made perfect?

MARCH 8

Today the fullness of God brings you to a new place. You will behold new things and have new experiences. You have been graced with the opportunity to do it again. There is an open door from God that allows you to have another opportunity to begin over. Grace provides this open door. Your slate has been wiped clean and God, through Christ Jesus has justified you. You have been given to the green light to start over again.

I prophesy to you that you will not waste any time dwelling on the past or the constituents that you have left behind. God has given you another chance and you must take full advantage of it. The new thing is here, and it has come for you. Be fully persuaded that what you have learned will be needed for what you are now walking in to.

Judges 16:28 - And Samson called unto the Lord, and said, O Lord God, remember me, I pray thee, and strengthen me, I pray thee, only this once, O God, that I may be at once avenged of the Philistines for my two eyes.

MARCH 9

Today the fullness of God brings you forth from the background to the front. Today you will feel the pull of God pulling you into a greater purpose. The Father pulls you into a greater awareness of His love for you. The Son pulls you into the purpose of your creation and the Holy Spirit pulls you into new realms of the Spirit. You are called upon by God to glorify Him in your life.

I prophesy to you today that you resist not the pull of God. This pulling comes from heaven, and you cannot deny it. It will pull on you until you obey. I speak to your will that you begin to go with God and cooperate with His will.

Psalms 31:4 - Pull me out of the net that they have laid privily for me: for thou art my strength.

MARCH 10

Today the trinity grants you authority to govern your affairs with a new grace. The Father teaches you how to manage your inheritance. The Son teaches you how to manage your ministry and the Holy Spirit teaches you how to manage your spirit. A greater ability to manage the things that have been given under your charge is with you now. You will not mismanage this season. You will know exactly what to do on the day to do it.

I prophesy to you today that you assume the reins of your life and properly administer it according to the will of God. You will not drop the ball. You will accomplish all that pertains to you. May you have good discernment to know what to do and how to do it. The grace of good stewardship is upon you.

Luke 12:42 - And the Lord said, Who then is that faithful and wise steward, whom his lord shall make ruler over his household, to give them their portion of meat in due season?

MARCH 11

Today is the day that the trinity breaks stubbornness off you. You have been resistant to the things that He has commanded you to do. You have allowed fear to lead you and govern your movements. But no more! The power of the full Godhead comes to deliver you from holding back and your unwillingness to submit to all He has ordained for you.

Today I prophesy to you that your hardened heart becomes a heart of flesh again. May you no longer allow the pain of the past to dictate your decision to move forward. I speak over your will and your heart that they both submit and surrender to the lordship of Jesus, and you give Him a full YES!

2 Timothy 4:18 - And the Lord shall deliver me from every evil work, and will preserve me unto his heavenly kingdom: to whom be glory for ever and ever. Amen.

MARCH 12

Today the trinity moves you according to divine authority. Heaven has declared your next move and the next place for you. God, in His fullness has determined the next place and the right pace of your life. God takes full authority and control of your affairs today. Give over to Him everything. He will oversee it all. He knows what you have need of before you even ask of Him.

Today I prophesy to you that you surrender the control of your entire life over to God. I speak to your level of trust in Him that it may increase more. Turn the wheel over to God for your life. He will guide you and take you to the right place. Trust Him and do not fear. All will be well.

Psalms 18:2 - The Lord is my rock, and my fortress, and my deliverer; my God, my strength, in whom I will trust; my buckler, and the horn of my salvation, and my high tower.

MARCH 13

Today you will experience the trinity revolting against everything that opposes you. Every opposition will be met with a heavenly uprising, which shall stand against it. Today God defends you and fights for you. There is a holy indignation that is present against the forces that bind you, hinder you and keep you held back. God wars against it today.

I prophesy to you that you will stand still and see the salvation of the Lord. You will not need to fight this, for the Lord your God fights for you. He pushes back all forces and powers that come to work against you. You cannot lose, for the Lord is with you.

Isaiah 59:19 - So shall they fear the name of the Lord from the west, and his glory from the rising of the sun. When the enemy shall come in like a flood, the Spirit of the Lord shall lift up a standard against him.

MARCH 14

The day of the trinity Passover is here. Today you will see how God in His fullness will grace you to live through turmoil. Pain and challenges will not have their way with you. You will survive what killed others. You will come through alive and well. The Lord causes death to pass over you.

I prophesy to you today that you make all the necessary sacrifices to God that will cause Him to do this work in your life. The Lord will not deny your sacrifices. He will not ignore what you place on the altar. Decide today to do what is necessary to appease God.

Psalms 91:10 - There shall no evil befall thee, neither shall any plague come nigh thy dwelling.

MARCH 15

Today you receive a greater ability to rest in the fact that God is with you. All of God is with you! He does not give you only parts or pieces of Himself, but His fullness is with you even now. This presence causes a divine rest to be upon you and with you. There is a security that comes upon you even now due to the knowing that all of God is with you. This places you to rest.

Today I prophesy to you that anxiety and fears no longer have a place in your life. The rest in knowing that God is with you calms your doubts and fears. I speak over your heart that you be settled, and your spirit be at peace because God is with you. Rest in knowing this.

Psalms 46:7 - The Lord of hosts is with us; the God of Jacob is our refuge. Selah.

MARCH 16

Today all the attributes of love surround you and fill you. Patience, kindness, supportive, humble, proper, good, promoting others, prayerful, celebration of truth, strong, faithful, enduring, unfailing are all attributes of love. And so, they are your attributes.

I prophesy to you today that you adapt the attributes of Love. I speak that you welcome what and who love fully is. Your life always reflects love. When you are low love lifts you. When you are empty, may love fill you. When you are lost, love will find you. The fullness of Love is with you, and you will know it.

John 15:12 - This is my commandment, That ye love one another, as I have loved you.

MARCH 17

Today the fullness of God aligns you with purpose and destiny. The answer to your reason for existence will be revealed today. Think it not strange concerning the things that occur today. For within it, God reveals why He placed you in the earth. You are a gift to the world and the things that are needed for you to walk fully into this are fully coming into order.

I prophesy that you fully cooperate with this alignment. I speak over you that the spirit like Abraham will follow through and willingly do what God asks of you. This yielding will release an order that you have been praying for and you will know it.

Genesis 22:9 - And they came to the place which God had told him of; and Abraham built an altar there, and laid the wood in order, and bound Isaac his son, and laid him on the altar upon the wood.

MARCH 18

Today the fullness of God breathes the breath of life into you. There is a resurrection and newness that occurs when God breathes. Today that same breath blows within you. Receive the breath of God. New life, Zoe and Pneuma is within you. Dead things come alive again. New things happen. Resuscitation and new creation are the order of the day for you.

I prophesy to you today that your nostrils be open and that you fully receive the fullness of God's breath within you. I speak that today you become a living soul that glorifies God in your life and body. You will lack nothing because the fullness of God is within you.

Genesis 2:7 - And the Lord God formed man of the dust of the ground, and breathed into his nostrils the breath of life; and man became a living soul.

MARCH 19

Today God makes the decision for you. You will no longer struggle between options. Your mind has been toiling between opinions on what to decide and how to approach situations. The Judgment of God is made known today as God decides for you. Heaven's rule will prevail above all other options and opinions. The case will be settled, and you will know the will of God.

I prophesy to you today that you walk in total agreement with what God decides for you. He knows what is best for you and He understands your needs. May your trust in Him increase more as you come to understand His ways. You will be better after this!

Proverbs 31:9 - Open thy mouth, judge righteously, and plead the cause of the poor and needy.

MARCH 20

Today you will walk in completeness. There is wholeness from heaven that is available to you today. God has released unto you the joy of being complete. There will be no voids or emptiness within you. Everything is complete. Those things that pertain to you are being completed as well. The Lord has done this for you, and you will reap the rewards of completion.

I prophesy to you today that you are total, whole, and complete. You are a complete person. You are the complete package. You are made whole. Healing has taken place and wholeness is the order of the day for you. It is time and this is the day for it to be made manifest within you.

Colossians 2:10 - And ye are complete in him, which is the head of all principality and power:

MARCH 21

Today the complete Godhead persuades you in His way. All the ways that you possess which are contrary to Him, God comes after. The Father, the Son and the Holy Spirit pull you into a new mindset and convince you to follow Him in every way. Your life will reflect His glory and presence and your will is changing to please Him more.

Today I prophesy that the feet of your mind begin to change course and direction. I speak that your will adjusts to the perfect will of God. You will begin to see a change in your habits, behaviors, and customs. They will all bow to the headship of God. It will be much better for you, and you will behold the blessings of transformation.

Proverbs 16:7 - When a man's ways please the Lord, he maketh even his enemies to be at peace with him.

MARCH 22

Today is a day of giving for you. The complete Godhead shares with you gifts from above. You will receive gifts from heaven and blessings will come your way. Not only will heaven give to you, but you will give to heaven and others. You will be a conduit for blessings and favor. Today the Lord uses you as a distribution center to disburse His blessings throughout the earth. You are a giver and God trusts you to give.

I prophesy to you today that your storehouse is full, and your barns press out with abundance. You will know no lack and overflow and outpour will be your norm. You are blessed to be a blessing. This is not for you to keep but to bless others. The more you bless others the more your blessings will flow.

Zechariah 8:13 - And it shall come to pass, that as ye were a curse among the heathen, O house of Judah, and house of Israel; so will I save you, and ye shall be a blessing: fear not, but let your hands be strong.

MARCH 23

Today God provides for you as His child. He reminds you that He loves you and that you are His. God wants you to know Him as Father! He is more than a provider and protector. He is the one who names you and your DNA comes from Him. God opens His arms to welcome you in His heart. He desires you to do the same as you come to Him. Receive your Father today. He Loves you.

I prophesy that you are healed from any issues you have had with your natural father. Those matters are affecting your relationship with God the Father. He has been looking for more from you and reaching for you, but your brokenness keeps Him at bay. Today you walk in healing & wholeness so that you may embrace the joy of your heavenly Father.

Matthew 6:26 - Behold the fowls of the air: for they sow not, neither do they reap, nor gather into barns; yet your heavenly Father feedeth them. Are ye not much better than they?

MARCH 24

Today the Holy Trinity brings you into a priestly order liken unto Melchizedek. This order is like no other order in that it is the order of God. God consecrates you and anoints you for such a time as this. This priestly order is an everlasting one. The sacrifices and prayers made are for eternity and have no end. Today God brings you into this order.

Today I prophesy to you that you begin to walk worthy of the grace that is upon your life. You will no longer simply bow to the will of man but to the sovereignty of God. There are priestly duties that you have been called to and you must fulfill them all. Today choose to give God a YES that He can use you in this way.

Psalms 110:4 - The Lord hath sworn, and will not repent, Thou art a priest for ever after the order of Melchizedek.

MARCH 25

Today you receive from the full Godhead multiplied blessings. What God has determined for you; you will receive it all. There will be no good thing withheld from you. Your capacity increases today to allow all that God has for you to come to you. Your vessels have been too few and your barrels are too shallow. The Lord increases your size so that you may receive the fullness of what heaven has ordered for you.

I prophesy to you today that you will not miss or lack anything that God desires for you. You have often felt left out, but God today reminds you that you have always been on His mind, and He has waited for the right time to release to you what He has. Today is that day. Receive it all!!

Psalms 84:11 - For the Lord God is a sun and shield: the Lord will give grace and glory: no good thing will he withhold from them that walk uprightly.

MARCH 26

Open your eyes and your heart today. You will behold God in His fullness. The complete Godhead wants to reveal to you what He has done for you and what He will do. You will see the image of God everywhere you go. God will appear to you in things that you will not expect. But it will be Him. Prepare to meet the Lord God today. This will reflect in many areas.

I prophesy to you today that you do not miss God. Your perception and intuition are purified to notice holy things. You will be able to distinguish the movements and the voice of God in many areas. You will see Him, you will hear Him, you will feel Him.

Genesis 32:30 - And Jacob called the name of the place Peniel: for I have seen God face to face, and my life is preserved.

MARCH 27

Today you will see what has taken place in eternity manifest in the earth. God the Father made us in the image of His son, Jesus Christ and has filled Him with His Spirit. This has been done so we can be redeemed and saved. The power of this work is manifested within you today. You will walk throughout the world as a living testimony of His saving grace. People will come to know the power of God through you.

I prophesy to you today that you be not ashamed of the power that you walk in. That you are not embarrassed or neglectful to tell others of the hope that lies within you. Heaven will speak to others through you. It will be a power that the earth has not seen since the resurrection of Christ.

Luke 9:26 - For whosoever shall be ashamed of me and of my words, of him shall the Son of man be ashamed, when he shall come in his own glory, and in his Father's, and of the holy angels.

MARCH 28

Today the full Godhead embraces you as His own. You are made in the likeness and the image of God. There is a grace that is upon you that others stand in awe of. It is the fullness of God within you. It causes you to complete tasks and manage difficult matters with seeming ease. Your execution is perceived perfect in the eyes of many. It is because the Lord is with you.

I prophesy to you today that you boast in the Lord of your accomplishments. Do not boast about yourself. But give all glory to God for the things that you have acquired and attained. This behavior will cause God to continuously use you and grant to you more. Humility is the way of righteousness.

James 1:25 - But whoso looketh into the perfect law of liberty, and continueth therein, he being not a forgetful hearer, but a doer of the work, this man shall be blessed in his deed.

MARCH 29

Today God makes you more adaptable for your next season. Things will begin to change around you. You will see a difference in many ways. But the Lord God will prepare you for the change that is happening. It will not catch you off guard. God begins to adjust within you now so that you are ready when it happens. Do not resist the changes; they are coming to make you ready for what is next.

Today I prophesy that you are more flexible with the things that are around you. You will not be tied to anything that is not eternal. God releases upon you a grace to change and be changed. When the season changes, so will you!

Hebrews 7:12 - For the priesthood being changed, there is made of necessity a change also of the law.

MARCH 30

Today is a good day for consecration. Separate yourself unto the Lord. The fullness of God desires to take you to another place in Him. He has more in store for you to do and accomplish. Your time is not up yet. Hollow out your life from among the others. There will be a distinction about you that is undeniable. God will use you in demonstration of power.

Today I prophesy to you that you seek the things that are above. As you devote your time to God in a greater way, you will see the proven power of God working through you. I speak into existence your new mindset and dedication to the things of God. It will produce fruitfulness in your life.

Exodus 32:29 - For Moses had said, Consecrate yourselves to day to the Lord, even every man upon his son, and upon his brother; that he may bestow upon you a blessing this day.

MARCH 31

Today the fullness of the Godhead calls you by His name. You will no longer carry the identity of the temporal, but you will be known by the identity of the Eternal. God places upon you, His name. Your identity will not be questioned or compromised. You will be known as His. He labels you so that the world and every other world will know that you are His. This identity will cover you for ages to come.

I prophesy to you today that you walk as god in the earth. You bear the name of the Lord. You are called by His name. Your behavior, habits and ways must be that of your Heavenly Father. You have His name. May your shoulders be broad to carry the weight of the responsibility of the name of God. Today you will know who you are!

Revelation 3:12 - Him that overcometh will I make a pillar in the temple of my God, and he shall go no more out: and I will write upon him the name of my God, and the name of the city of my God, which is new Jerusalem, which cometh down out of heaven from my God: and I will write upon him my new name.

APRIL

"The Month of The Winds (Earth)"

APRIL 1

Today the winds testify of God. You will flow into new revelation of God. God blows fresh winds of glory and power in your direction. Do not be fooled. All power belongs to God. Even when the wind blows upon another, it is God who sends the wind. You will receive power after the Holy Ghost has come upon you and you will be a witness for Him

I prophesy to you today that you tap into a new flow of God. There is a new flow that you will be graced to move into. It comes from God, and he releases it in your life today. Embrace it and welcome the winds of change blowing in your life.

Ecclesiastes 1:6 - The wind blows to the south and goes around to the north; around and around goes the wind, and on its circuits the wind returns.

APRIL 2

Today you will witness the winds blowing in your favor. You will experience a gust of glory coming your way. The north wind will bring you stability and fortitude. The south wind will bring to you fire and zeal. The west wind will blow to you rest and peace and the east wind will blow to you glory and presence. The winds will show you the will of God for your life.

Today I prophesy to you that you fully embrace what the Lord is doing and sending in your life. May you inhale that which is blowing in your direction. God cause you to behold new things and its coming through the winds of heaven.

Luke 12:55 - And when ye see the south wind blow, ye say, There will be heat; and it cometh to pass.

APRIL 3

The wind of God comes to fill you today. All that you will need for the next assignment will come with this new breeze. It is a rushing mighty wind. It will fill you and make you full. It will empower you and consecrate you. The wind that the Lord sends today will come through prayer and fasting. As you separate yourself from others, God will blow into you an anointing that sets you on fire.

Today I prophesy to you that you walk as a disciple of the Lord chosen for this time. May you walk circumspectly in the world as a vessel of God doing great exploits. You are not just a bystander; you are a vessel unto His glory and honor.

Acts 2:2 - And suddenly there came a sound from heaven as of a rushing mighty wind, and it filled all the house where they were sitting.

APRIL 4

Today the winds blow from all over the earth towards you. There is a gust of blessings and provision that the Lord sends in your direction. You will experience it all around you. You will not be able to escape it. It will be overwhelming for you to receive. You do not have enough room. Every time you turn around there will be another blessing in store for you.

Today I prophesy to you that you will collect the blessings that God has for you. They are innumerable and they come from all directions. They are the blessings from God, and they make you rich and no sadness will be with it.

Deuteronomy 28:2 - And all these blessings shall come upon you and overtake you, if you obey the voice of the Lord your God.

APRIL 5

Today the wind of favor blows in your direction. What your money could not afford, favor will pay for. God will cause His favor to follow you. You are flavored with His favor, and you will not be denied of the blessing. Supernatural favor flows towards you today. God has commanded it to do so.

I prophesy to you today that you walk in uncommon favor for what you need in business, your family and even ministry. May unexpected phone calls and emails come to you to bless you and give you what you need. You will testify that the Lord has done this thing for me.

Luke 1:28 - And the angel came in unto her, and said, Hail, thou that art highly favoured, the Lord is with thee: blessed art thou among women.

APRIL 6

Today God sends you help. He causes people who are well skilled and equipped to come into your life. They will assist in the assignments that you have been given. God sends you help to build, help to gather, help to grow, and help to manage. The Lord of the harvest sends laborers for your vineyard.

I prophesy to you today that the right people will not miss you and the wrong people cannot find you. I speak into your life trusted vessels of honor who will support your endeavors and help you to manage the life God has given you.

Psalms 20:2 - Send thee help from the sanctuary, and strengthen thee out of Zion;

APRIL 7

Today the wind of perfection blows your way. You will perfectly complete every assignment given to you in this season. God grants you the maturity to oversee every task and to finish it. The Lord sends you help that empowers you to close all open projects. Today you flow in perfect timing, perfect strength, and perfect peace. It will all be accomplished.

I prophesy to you today that you operate like a well-oiled machine. The right answers flow out of you. The right mindset is within you and the right heart beats within you. There is a maturity about you that causes you to ignore the nay-sayers and focus on your assignment. They will not distract you from what you are called to do.

Deuteronomy 32:4 - He is the Rock, his work is perfect: for all his ways are judgment: a God of truth and without iniquity, just and right is he.

APRIL 8

Today the winds blow newness into your life. That which was old and done away with is no longer for you. There is a newness that comes upon you. As the flowers bloom and grow so will you experience new things in your life. This wind blows out the old things. The dead leaves and dead things are drifting away. But the new things rise to the surface, and you rise with them.

I prophesy to you today that you have a new perspective and a new focus. The new things that have been determined for you do now happen. New is the order of the day. New is what you receive and new is who you are.

Psalms 147:18 - He sendeth out his word, and melteth them: he causeth his wind to blow, and the waters flow.

APRIL 9

Today the winds break through the tough areas of your life. God causes the wind to blow and the things that would not seem to break will be broken. The force of this winds causes things to break and be destroyed because God sends this wind. That which was tough and stubborn will now back up to the gust of wind that heaven sends your way.

I prophesy to you today that you be more stable than ever. When the wind comes it will blow everything that is not stable. You must be established in God to survive this next wind. Plant your feet today. There is a wind that is blowing.

1 Chronicles 16:30 - Fear before him, all the earth: the world also shall be stable, that it be not moved.

APRIL 10

Today God sends the wind of authority into your life. Today you have the authority to command a blessing and the winds will take what you speak and carry it to manifestation. Your words carry weight as the heavens bring divine support to your speech. Watch your words today because everything you say will be bought to pass.

I prophesy to you today that your voice echoes the sentiments of heaven. Your tone, your articulation and your language are all anointed to create. You will live on the level you speak. May your language be clear to line up with the will of God.

Romans 4:17 - (As it is written, I have made thee a father of many nations,) before him whom he believed, even God, who quickeneth the dead, and calleth those things which be not as though they were.

APRIL 11

Today the wind of heaven blows out everything that is not like God from within you. Wind not only comes to blow things in, but it blows things away. Everything that is not like God will be carried away. There is a storm coming that will do away with all the things that displease Him. You will begin to see a change within you as your character shifts with the wind for the better.

I prophesy to you today that you allow God to work a work in you. You give permission to the Spirit of Grace to make you better and drive away those things that you have held on to. You will be satisfied when the Lord has completed this work in you.

Genesis 32:24 - And Jacob was left alone; and there wrestled a man with him until the breaking of the day.

APRIL 12

Today the shifting winds blow in your direction. This wind shifts you into apostolic authority. Divine order goes with you today. God has ordered this day and ordered your steps. You are ordained to have prosperity, healing, and joy. This is your inheritance as a believer. God grants you the order of His spirit and brings all tings into alignment with His will.

Today I prophesy to you that you walk with apostolic authority in the earth declaring the riches of God truth. Your fruit will be everlasting joy and life. Every opposing force must submit to this authority and obey your voice.

Luke 10:17 - And the seventy returned again with joy, saying, Lord, even the devils are subject unto us through thy name.

APRIL 13

Today rebellion is broken by the wind of God. All the things your flesh has protested, will bow to the sovereignty of God. Our nature resists His will, but God knows how to get to us. Today is the day where He comes for those things within you that resist His will. You must surrender and submit, and you will see the rewards of your deliverance.

I prophesy to you today that you walk in humility and that pride is broken off you. There is a magnificent work to be done in you and God is prepared to do it. May your will bow to His power and may you receive this next gust of breakthrough in your personal life.

Romans 8:7 - Because the carnal mind is enmity against God: for it is not subject to the law of God, neither indeed can be.

APRIL 14

Today the winds blow calamity, unrest, and chaos past you. There is a covering protection that hides you. The blood of Jesus Christ defends you from all harm. The wind that blows in the earth to judge, call out and chasten others will pass you. Sickness, poverty, destruction and even death will not be your portion. But health, prosperity, joy, and life will follow you.

I prophesy to you today that you remain covered under the divine protection of God. Do not remove yourself from the sacred covering of His voice and His will. God has determined that this time must come for others, but it will not come near you.

Psalms 20:1 - May the LORD answer you in the day of trouble! May the name of the God of Jacob protect you!

APRIL 15

Today God blows you into a rest. The Lord causes you to abide in Him so that you may be the recipient of His peace to rest. He desires to refresh you and rejuvenate you. You will rest in His will and his loving embrace. It is a Sabbath for you. Your mind, your spirit and even your body will rest today.

I prophesy to you today that you order your schedule to rest. I command you to make the time to steal away and retreat with the Father. No matter what the responsibilities are, it is your responsibility to enter a rest that God may minister to you.

Hebrews 4:9 - There remaineth therefore a rest to the people of God.

APRIL 16

God's love covers you like the winds blow in the earth. When the winds blow, you do not know where it comes from or where it is going. But it touches everything that is in its path. This is how the Love of God will cover you today. You will not expect it or see it, but it will touch you in a very deep way. You cannot avoid it or resist it. The wind of His love will find you today and bring you comfort and peace.

Today I prophesy to you that you welcome the wind of His love and be comforted by it. May you walk in divine love. May your mind grow in trust in the Lord that you may receive the love that He has for you.

John 3:8 - The wind bloweth where it listeth, and thou hearest the sound thereof, but canst not tell whence it cometh, and whither it goeth: so is every one that is born of the Spirit.

APRIL 17

Today the wind of God aligns you with your purpose and destiny. Be prepared to make moves today that will set your life in a path for the next several years to come. There is a holy alignment that comes today for you and there is a rush to get you there. God prepares the way for you, and he makes all things possible.

I prophesy to you today that you follow and flow with the wind of God that brings you into a place of purpose. You will not be lost or unclear concerning your assignment on the earth. Clarity comes with this wind. Simply trust and obey and you will eat the fat of the land.

Isaiah 40:4 - Every valley shall be exalted, and every mountain and hill shall be made low: and the crooked shall be made straight, and the rough places plain:

APRIL 18

Today the earth yields life to you. No more dead things shall be named among you. Life is your reward. There is a resurrection of things that have died. There is a force of life that comes upon you. All deadly things are rebuked and cast out. You are compelled by God to LIVE!

I prophesy to you today that you decide in your soul to live. No matter what the news or the challenges you face. With God all things are possible. You can come through anything with Him. May you have a desire more than ever before to live to see the future you have been promised.

1 Timothy 6:12 - Fight the good fight of faith, lay hold on eternal life, whereunto thou art also called, and hast professed a good profession before many witnesses.

APRIL 19

Today is the day that the wind of God blows strong discernment within you. You will possess the mind of God and you will think as He does. His mind fills your mind today that you may make decisions that please Him. The Lord will directly influence your choices. You will make the right decisions. Trust in Him who will lead you into the right path. He will direct you with His wind.

I prophesy to you today that you make godly judgments and that your mind bows to the mind of God. May you be delivered in the spirit of your mind and possess the mind of Christ.

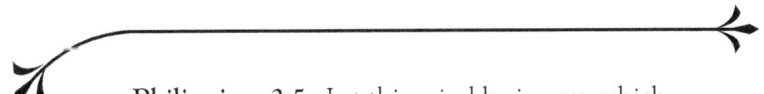

Philippians 2:5 - Let this mind be in you, which was also in Christ Jesus:

APRIL 20

Today the wind of the Lord causes you to redeem the time you have wasted. All the time you were doing what you desired but it did not line up with the will of God, God will cause that time to double and come back to you. He is adding years to your life. There is a completeness that comes to you today of a cycle so that redemption may begin.

Today I prophesy to you that you begin to collect the minutes, hours, days, weeks, months, and the years that have been left behind for you to fulfill your purpose. The strength of your youth returns to you. You will begin to walk in the wisdom of your years but run in the power of your youth.

Joel 2:25 - And I will restore to you the years that the locust hath eaten, the cankerworm, and the caterpiller, and the palmerworm, my great army which I sent among you.

APRIL 21

Today God blows the scales from off your eyes and removes the blinders off your mind to see those who come to do wickedness to you. Your enemies are being revealed. Those who have been working against you will be made known. God send the winds of heaven to blow the curtains back and cause you to walk in complete awareness of those who are for you.

I prophesy to you today that you possess divine wisdom on how to manage challenging situations in relationships. I speak a divine strategy be released that causes you to speak, think and behave in a wise and perfect way. You will not be unseemly, but graciously you will oversee every situation with poise.

Psalms 101:2 - I will behave myself wisely in a perfect way. O when wilt thou come unto me? I will walk within my house with a perfect heart.

APRIL 22

Today the wind blows happiness towards you. God makes you happy in Him. You will possess a peace and joy that cannot be quenched. God causes you to know His will for you and His desires for your life. You find happiness in pleasing Him. Your joy will be full and your heart content with His plans for you.

Today I prophesy to you that you choose to be happy. All the things that bring you unrest are cast away and there is an embrace for the things that complete you. Welcome happiness... it is Gods will for you.

Habakkuk 3:18 - Yet I will rejoice in the Lord, I will joy in the God of my salvation.

APRIL 23

Today the wind produces an increase for you. Your capacity to stretch and your ability to receive is increasing. God causes you to produce and be productive in every way. No longer will you think on a limited level. But now you will function with a limitless mindset. God brings you into an abundant thinking.

I prophesy to you today that you allow your mind and heart to extend to another place in God. May you produce more success, more favor, and more joy. I speak productivity upon you at a rate that will amaze you.

Joshua 5:12 - And the manna ceased on the morrow, after they had eaten of the produce of the land; neither had the children of Israel manna any more; but they did eat of the fruit of the land of Canaan that year.

APRIL 24

Today the anointing of God is upon you to affect the world. The north, south, east, and west of you will hear your voice and receive your words and wisdom. God gives you a grace to meet needs and destroy yokes that binds others. You have been anointed for a greater region than your present location. Other people from other regions are seeking you out. God has given you what they need.

Today I prophesy to you that you submit to being used of God to serve a greater circumference. Your territory of reach is growing, and the Lord will use you to bless and serve. Prepare for the anointing to be with you for many days.

Isaiah 61:1 - The Spirit of the Lord God is upon me; because the Lord hath anointed me to preach good tidings unto the meek; he hath sent me to bind up the brokenhearted, to proclaim liberty to the captives, and the opening of the prison to them that are bound;

APRIL 25

Today there is another grace that comes upon you by the wind of God. You have been comfortable operating on a familiar level and in a familiar place. But today God begins to breathe upon you a new grace that enables you to do more and greater. You will not operate in a common place any longer. But you will be as effective and even more effective in demonstration.

I prophesy to you today that you accept the grace of God given to you for this hour. God will get the glory out of your life, and you will walk in His supernatural power. It will not be you, but Him working within you. Accept what He is doing through you.

Acts 4:33 - And with great power gave the apostles witness of the resurrection of the Lord Jesus: and great grace was upon them all.

APRIL 26

Today the earth will testify of God's existence to you. The heavens will declare His glory and goodness. You will behold the beauty of His majesty and your eyes will see His goodness. The skilled work of His hands will be evident to you, and it will cause you to praise Him even more. Trees, land, flowers, and the sea will all reveal to you the sovereignty and great power of God. You will be in awe of how much He is able to do.

Today I prophesy that you will not miss the majesty of His creation. I say that you will not only see it in the earth, but you will also see it within you. Your eyes will behold the handiwork of God in your own image, and you will be satisfied at His creation.

Psalms 8:1 - To the chief Musician upon Gittith, A Psalm of David. O Lord our Lord, how excellent is thy name in all the earth! who hast set thy glory above the heavens.

APRIL 27

Today the winds blow a saving grace to you. The presence of God not only protects and defends you, but it spares you from devastation. Today the wind of God causes you to avoid that which would be detrimental. This is a decision of God. Though you may be in harm's way, the Lord knows your steps and He is aware of what is ahead. He sees what you do not see.

I prophesy to you today that you are completely covered by Him, who no one and nothing can surpass. I speak into you long life and extended living. You will not fall victim of catastrophe because it is the Lord God who saves you. Be saved from all that harms you.

Psalms 106:47 - Save us, O Lord our God, and gather us from among the heathen, to give thanks unto thy holy name, and to triumph in thy praise.

APRIL 28

Today there is a wind of assistance that rests upon you to walk in excellence. Mediocrity and normalcy have been removed from your heart and mind. You are being given a mind that strives for a greater and a more perfect way. Your desires are shifting to a higher life. Your thoughts are being elevated to another dimension. It is God who causes you to think as He does.

I prophetically declare over your life that you will operate in the realm of a high life. You now walk in such excellence that low level living is clearly identified and done away with. God grants you favor of stewardship that you may be able to show forth His Glory in the earth.

Ephesians 2:6 - and raised us up with him and seated us with him in the heavenly places in Christ Jesus,

APRIL 29

Today the winds of change are blowing in your direction. There is a divine adjustment that is taking place which will catapult you into your future. God begins to cause such a transformation in your life that will bear fruit in every area. This is the change of God. This is the change you have been waiting for. It is here. It is today. Change happens within you.

I prophesy to you today that you welcome what is happening beginning today. Though it may last for the next couple of months, what begins today will have lasting results. Open your heart to what God is doing now. It will produce the things you have been praying for.

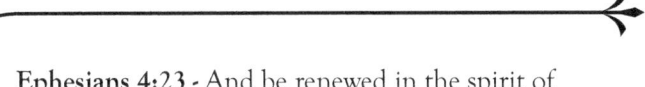

Ephesians 4:23 - And be renewed in the spirit of your mind;

APRIL 30

Today the Lord breaths His breathe of consecration upon you. This causes you to be separated from others that are around you. You have been chosen for a special work in the earth and the Lord's desire is to prepare you for it. You have been molded for this hour. He wants you to Himself so that He may minister to you what will come to pass. This is the hour of consecration where you must part from others so that you may be used by Him.

I speak prophetically in your life that you willing to obey God in this season of consecration. This will require a mature mind and heart. You will be released into new realms of revelation and knowledge. Do not resist the wind of God that blows upon you today that causes you to be compelled to pray, fast, and spend quality time with God.

2 Corinthians 6:17 - Wherefore come out from among them, and be ye separate, saith the Lord, and touch not the unclean thing; and I will receive you,

MAY

"The Month of Grace and Favor"

MAY 1

Today the favor of God rests upon you. This is no ordinary favor, but that which comes straight from the throne of God. He gives you the ability to acquire what you cannot afford. He Favors you with the abundance of heaven. You will walk in supernatural favor today. Not only to acquire things, but also to obtain favorable opportunities. Doors you may not be qualified for are opening to you today. The Lord shines His favor on you.

I prophesy to you that people will begin to bless you. The stranger will find you to be a blessing to you. The favor of God upon you is undeniable. Do not neglect to glorify Him and praise His name for the remarkable things that are happening in your life.

Philippians 4:19 - But my God shall supply all your need according to his riches in glory by Christ Jesus.

MAY 2

Today you will witness the Grace of God on your life, ministry, and business. There is an enablement that you will possess that makes difficult tasks seem simple. It is the grace of God! Others will be in awe and amazement as to the things you will be able to accomplish with little resources. God is your source and with Him, all things are possible.

Today I prophesy to you that you will begin to settle your spirit from all anxiety and fear. I speak to your mind that you accept the grace that is upon you to get the job done. You have been anointed for now and you will walk in grace to do great exploits in the earth. You will glorify God in your body, soul, and spirit.

2 Corinthians 8:9 - For ye know the grace of our Lord Jesus Christ, that, though he was rich, yet for your sakes he became poor, that ye through his poverty might be rich.

MAY 3

Today the full godhead favors you with abundance. You will begin to see an overwhelming river of resources flow in your direction. Be prepared to be overtaken by the blessings of provision. There will be no lack among you. You will have and possess more than enough. Today live and walk in the abundant favor of God.

I prophesy to you today that you are wise to properly steward the abundance that is coming your way. The copious blessing will require that you manage the provision of God with the heart of Joseph. I speak the heart of Joseph within you so that you may manage the blessings of the Lord and yet maintain a heart that pursues Him with passion.

Nehemiah 9:25 - And they took strong cities, and a fat land, and possessed houses full of all goods, wells digged, vineyards, and oliveyards, and fruit trees in abundance: so they did eat, and were filled, and became fat, and delighted themselves in thy great goodness.

MAY 4

There is a grace in the earth that causes men to know God. You possess that grace. You are one of the vessels the Lord has anointed to carry the gospel message throughout the world. God has graced you with salvation and now He gives you the aptitude to share His love with everyone you meet. You will begin to travel and meet new people, which will be opportunities to spread the love of God.

I prophesy to you today that you function with holy boldness to operate in the grace given to you. I declare that you will not be ashamed to speak up concerning the things of God and His kingdom. You will witness to others, and they will be aware of the saving Grace of God through Jesus Christ.

Ephesians 3:8 - Unto me, who am less than the least of all saints, is this grace given, that I should preach among the Gentiles the unsearchable riches of Christ;

MAY 5

Today double favor follows you and flows through you. Today God grants to you the portion that is due you as well as the portion of others. There is a kindness that heaven expresses to you that others will know that God has smiled upon you. You will have the double portion of God. Do not deny yourself the blessings of His favor.

I speak prophetically to you that you welcome through your mind and behavior all that God has prepared for you. Allow the favor to have her perfect work in you and do what the Lord has commanded her to do in your life.

Zechariah 9:12 - Turn you to the strong hold, ye prisoners of hope: even to day do I declare that I will render double unto thee;

MAY 6

Today you will witness the favor of partnerships, friendships, and companionships. The Lord God begins to eliminate all the relationships of your life that does not bring Him glory and you closer to your purpose. There is a cleansing of affiliations that God begins to do. There are fresh connections and new networks that are flowing in your direction. That which seemed too difficult to get into, you will be now invited into. The favor of God for these new interactions has come.

Today I prophesy to you that you welcome the new partners in business, the new friendships in your life. I speak healing over you and within you from the hurt of the past. May you trust and love again so that whom God has for you next may be able to come into your life and enjoy your company without the charge of the past.

Ecclesiastes 4:9 - Two are better than one; because they have a good reward for their labour.

MAY 7

Today you possess the grace to complete all things in your life that have been left undone. Not only will you complete tasks, but you will do so with excellence. There is a grace upon you to have closure on all open events, tasks, and responsibilities. Your bills, job responsibilities and your home will all have closure on things you need to have done.

I prophesy today that you complete the assignment given to you. You will have sufficiency of strength and resources to do so. God is with you. Your mind and body are sharp and strong. I speak your goals met and your aspirations obtained.

You must and you will finish this.

Luke 14:28 - For which of you, intending to build a tower, sitteth not down first, and counteth the cost, whether he have sufficient to finish it?

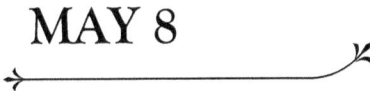

MAY 8

Today is the day that you have the favor of a new start. God wipes your slate clean and gives you the opportunity to start all over. Through the blessing of justification, God does not look at your past. He does not charge it to you because of the sacrifice of Jesus Christ. You now have a chance to begin again. Today you experience new mercies.

I prophesy today that you take full advantage of the grace given to you to start over. This is your do-over season. God allows you to flow in the things you missed in your past and to accomplish what you failed at before. May you take full possession of this blessing and spend your time wisely.

Hebrews 10:20 - By a new and living way, which he hath consecrated for us, through the veil, that is to say, his flesh;

MAY 9

Today the things that has you bound is loosed from off you. You are graced to walk in new realms of deliverance and breakthrough. No longer will you struggle in your flesh with the things that takes you away from the purpose and will of God. God gives you the grace to walk out of the places that once had you imprisoned. You are being made free from mental, physical, and emotional hindrances.

I speak prophetically into you that you welcome the deliverance that God has for you and that you come into full agreement with your breakthrough. Surrender to the will of God and accept the salvation that He offers you.

Galatians 5:1 - Stand fast therefore in the liberty wherewith Christ hath made us free, and be not entangled again with the yoke of bondage.

MAY 10

Today you walk in the favor of influence in the earth. Because of the anointing on your life, the Lord gives you influence with communities that you are called to. You will rise to be a leading voice in the areas of your influences. You will be sought after and called upon to give direction and wisdom in areas that you have been graced to affect.

I prophesy today that you walk in the wisdom of your influence. May you never lord over the people that God gives you, but may you, with humility, bless those who listen to you and call upon you. May you gain influence increasingly and may you come before great men.

Proverbs 18:16 - A man's gift maketh room for him, and bringeth him before great men.

MAY 11

Today, God graces you with healing. He fills all the voids in your heart that cause you to feel incomplete. You have been warring with issues of your past and you have been toiling with the trauma of yesterday. But today God begins the powerful work of healing in your life that you no longer feel unfinished within yourself. Your feelings of inadequacies are over.

I prophesy to you today wholeness. You are being made whole today from the crown of your head to the soles of your feet. Every part of you is being graced to be intact and unbroken. May your heart experience the favor of wholeness and may you begin to be healed in your perception.

Job 5:18 - For he maketh sore, and bindeth up: he woundeth, and his hands make whole.

MAY 12

Today you possess the favor of divine order. All things that were out of the order of God for your life are now surrendering to a holy order. Before you came into being the Lord ordered your steps and your life. Life challenges have taken you off course. But the Lord is now causing the authority of heaven to reposition you back in place. God takes full control of your way, your life, and your next steps.

I speak prophetically to you today of what God is doing in you. I speak that you bow to His sovereignty and power. May you submit to the shifting of the Lord that puts you under His rule and brings you into total alignment with His will.

1 Corinthians 15:24 - Then cometh the end, when he shall have delivered up the kingdom to God, even the Father; when he shall have put down all rule and all authority and power.

MAY 13

Today you possess the grace to resist the devil and all his plans. You gain a greater fight to oppose the temptations of the evil one that causes you to rebel and disobey God's will. Your struggles have been strong, but today God gives you a greater strength from heaven to push back the will to go in the wrong direction. Your fight increases today.

I prophesy to you today that you begin to revolt against the will to step outside of the will of God. May you oppose every force and suggestion to anything else other than what God has permitted for you. Be strengthened today to stand tall in the deliverance you now possess.

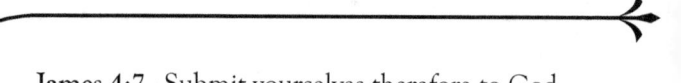

James 4:7 - Submit yourselves therefore to God. Resist the devil, and he will flee from you.

MAY 14

Today God favors you with what does not happen. The favor of God is not just for what is given to you, but also what is not given to you. This is called the mercy of God. The Lord has mercy on you today and causes the penalty that was due to you, to pass by you. You will begin to see favor in a new light of mercy. The Lord will not allow the pains of the day to befall you. Sacrifices will make this possible.

I prophesy to you today that you as you make a sacrifice to the Lord today that He will cause you to live. Life is His will for you. He will bring you to a greater level of awareness of His will for you that will compel you to offer up to Him praise He is worthy of and sacrifices that please Him. This act releases his favor of prevention.

2 Peter 3:9 - The Lord is not slack concerning his promise, as some men count slackness; but is longsuffering to us-ward, not willing that any should perish, but that all should come to repentance.

MAY 15

Today you have the grace of rest. The spirit of aggravation and frustration is being rebuked off you. You will not be in a place of unrest. You will find your heart settled and your mind at peace. God does a splendid work in your life that causes you to be tranquil and worry free.

I prophesy a calmness to come over your life like a mighty river. No matter what you are faced with today or in this season, you will remain in a state of rest. May you be assured of the presence of the Lord with you and His ability to manage what you cannot.

Matthew 11:29 - Take my yoke upon you, and learn of me; for I am meek and lowly in heart: and ye shall find rest unto your souls.

MAY 16

Today you receive the favor of God's love. He loves you with an everlasting love. His love for you is unfailing and uncompromised. He loves you without condition and regardless of if you love Him in return, He yet loves you. God expresses a love to you that you have never experienced before. This is favorable for you because you need His love. His love is the presence in your life that keeps you going.

Today I prophesy that you are overtaken by the favor of Gods love. May you meet every moment in this day with the favor of His love. May you walk with your head held high knowing the God lives you and He will not change His mind concerning you.

Jeremiah 31:3 - The Lord hath appeared of old unto me, saying, Yea, I have loved thee with an everlasting love: therefore with lovingkindness have I drawn thee.

MAY 17

Today you walk in the grace of alignment with the things of the Spirit. All the things that were misaligned are now lining up with what God has ordered for you. The things you have prayed for and were lacking are coming into manifestation. The order of God has been determined for you and has come to pass.

I prophesy to you today that your feet begin to move according to this new alignment with the Spirit of grace. May your feet be swift, and your footing be sure. I rebuke slothful feet and I send to you a fire to make your feel move swiftly in the things of God. Be aligned with God today.

Psalms 18:33 - He maketh my feet like hinds' feet, and setteth me upon my high places.

MAY 18

Today God graces you to live! There is a new determination upon you to live. Death and dying goes far from you. You have been given a drive like never before. Life is abundantly available for you to live. God gives you a grace to allow you to experience this life to please Him and show others His love and kindness.

I prophesy to you a new exuberance and excitement about life. Whereas nothing special needs to occur, but there is a natural enthusiasm within you when it comes to living your best life before God. This grace comes with joy and peace. It is the God life (Zoe) that you are now living.

Proverbs 16:15 - In the light of the king's countenance is life; and his favour is as a cloud of the latter rain.

MAY 19

Today God makes a judgment concerning you. He decides to grace you. God gives you the benefits of joy, peace, and life due to His own will for you. Because of Jesus Christ His son, God has decided to bless you and keep you in His hand. Nothing can change His mind about you. He has made this judgment and it is His alone to decide. You are the recipient of the rich grace of God that you did not earn, nor can you pay for. The efficacious blood of Jesus has paid it for.

I prophesy to you today that you forever remember the grace that God has decided to grant you. That you are in eternal commemoration of what the Lord has done for you. With that memory, may you tell others of His love for you. May you be an eternal witness of the kindness of God.

James 4:6 - But he gives more grace. Therefore it says, "God opposes the proud but gives grace to the humble."

MAY 20

Today you have been given the grace to complete a cycle of trauma in your life. For too long you have been gripped by the strength of the things that happened in your past. They have warped your perception and have imprisoned your destiny. But today grace unlocks the door of your mind and allows you to grab hold of what has been waiting on you. You will no longer live in fear and the vicious cycles of anniversaries that remind you of what happened are now over.

I prophesy healing to you today. I speak into your spirit the boldness to chase after the balm of restoration that puts you back in the place where you belong. I prophesy to your mind that you are strong enough to withstand the suggestions of failure in order that you might receive the promise of success.

Psalms 34:4 - I sought the Lord, and he heard me,
and delivered me from all my fears.

MAY 21

Today is the day when God gives you the grace to heal yourself. You have been self-sabotaging your future because deep down you have lost hope. You no longer see any further than where you are and what you possess. But the enemy has lied to you. Today you begin to break the willfulness you have had to embrace the lie. God grants you the grace to see things further, deeper, and better than you have ever done so before.

I prophesy to your mind that everything that agrees with the lie you have heard is broken and dismantled. I speak to your eyes that you begin to see further and clearer than ever before. The grace of God is with you for this hour. Begin to heal yourself.

Luke 4:23 - And he said unto them, Ye will surely say unto me this proverb, Physician, heal thyself: whatsoever we have heard done in Capernaum, do also here in thy country.

MAY 22

Today the favor of good pleasure is upon you and with you. You will walk in abundant happiness. The spirit of glee is with you, and you will not be able to shake it. It is joyous to even be around you. Sadness, sorrow, and grief have gone far from you as the east is to the west. God send supernatural joy to you, and it follows you wherever you go.

I prophesy to you today that you spread this joy and happiness to others. I prophesy that you are a joy distributor. Others will find it a joy to be around you and desire to fellowship with you. I tell you that your joy is full and complete, and it is a deep well that others will be able to draw from.

2 Thessalonians 1:11 - Wherefore also we pray always for you, that our God would count you worthy of this calling, and fulfil all the good pleasure of his goodness, and the work of faith with power:

MAY 23

Today is the day the grace and favor reproduce after its kind. The seeds of grace and favor are now multiplied in your life and there is more of it available for you. Grace produces favor and favor produces grace. You will never be without the choice blessings of God in your life because of this algorithm. God has designed it that every time you exhaust grace and favor, another harvest of more is immediately available.

I prophesy today that you show others the same grace and favor that God has shown you. You are the recipient of free gifts and now you must share these gifts freely. Your kindness will not only show your unselfishness, but it will show the glory of God in your life. As you do this, it produces even more.

Romans 4:16 - Therefore it is of faith, that it might be by grace; to the end the promise might be sure to all the seed; not to that only which is of the law, but to that also which is of the faith of Abraham; who is the father of us all,

MAY 24

Today is a day that God graces you with a visitation and He favors you to speak to you concerning what will be. The voice of the Lord comes to you to reveal to you how He will use you and get glory out of your life. There is an assignment that you will be given that will play a role in many coming to know the Lord. Only do not doubt or fear. Do not speak against what the Lord is doing in this season. As you send up prayers today, God will speak loudly what He desires to do.

I prophesy today that you speak only what the Lord is speaking. May everything you speak be an echo if what God has already spoken. As a believer, your words will bear fruit and it is crucial that you only say what God is saying. As you do this, the plan of God will be revealed more and more. You will have everlasting Joy because of this.

Luke 1:8 - And it came to pass, that while he executed the priest's office before God in the order of his course,

MAY 25

Today is the day that you possess the grace to entreat God for His favor. Whatever you ask for, it will be given to you. The Lord bends His ear to you and listens for your petitions. As you seek Him and make your requests known, God will answer speedily. Today is the day that your faith in prayer is built. You will be greeted by heaven with multiplied grace.

I prophesy to you today that you continuously build yourself up to pray. God will meet you in the hour of prayer to speak to you and fellowship with you. Your prayer time is valuable to God, and He will grace you with the favor that only heaven can give.

John 15:7 - If you abide in me, and my words abide in you, ask whatever you wish, and it will be done for you.

MAY 26

Today there is grace released for you to see the image of God in your life. You will possess a discernment to be able to know what God is doing and where God is. You will have a great level of clarity. The enemy will not be able to fool you with trickery and deception. The Lord has released a grace to you that is able to detect Him.

Today I prophesy that you use this grace to glorify God. When you see the Lord moving, tell others where He is. You will be a sign to others as a way of God. You will point the way and they will follow. God anoints you for this and you have been called to this.

Job 19:26 - And though after my skin worms destroy this body, yet in my flesh shall I see God:

MAY 27

Today you will enjoy the grace of salvation. God sent His son Jesus Christ into the world to give His life as a ransom for your soul. This selfless act of sacrifice has given you a gift of salvation that comes with countless benefits. Today those benefits are evident in your life. You now have life and that more abundantly. You possess Joy that is unspeakable Not as the world gives, but as only God gives to you. Salvation has many rewards and benefits; the ultimate is eternal life. Today you begin to enjoy it all.

I prophesy today that you begin to enjoy the grace of salvation and the joy it brings. I say that your yokes are easy, and your burdens be light. May all the profits that salvation has to offer flow to you today and may you relish them all with gladness.

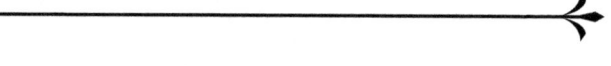

Isaiah 12:3 - Therefore with joy shall ye draw water out of the wells of salvation.

MAY 28

Today you will experience the favor of precision. You have been attempting to reach a goal and hit a certain target in your life and seemingly you keep missing. But today the Lord favors you with precision in the spirit that you may be able to accomplish your goals with accuracy. There is a meticulousness that comes upon you, which causes you to pay attention to details you have once missed. God has graced you to be more exact in ways you have never been before.

I prophesy today that you become an expert shooter in the spirit that even when you pray, you not only hit the target, but you get answers more quickly. I tell you that your attention to minute details will yield you greater rewards of accomplishment and perfection.

1 Corinthians 9:25 - And every man that striveth for the mastery is temperate in all things. Now they do it to obtain a corruptible crown; but we an incorruptible.

MAY 29

Today God graces you to evolve further into the greatness that He has ordained. You have been growing, changing, and being transformed daily by the Lord. Today you will begin to see the results of this change and what you are becoming. The Lord is not through with you, but you are progressing greatly. Do not be afraid of the changes that are being made. They are all working together for your good.

Today I prophesy to you that you begin to change even the more into what God has called you to be. I speak of a divine transformation that will cause others to look at you in amazement of your new development. You will not resemble the opposition or challenges you have been made to face. You will only look like the victory that you possess.

Psalms 18:19 - He brought me forth also into a large place; he delivered me, because he delighted in me.

MAY 30

Today the grace of wisdom is with you. You will walk in a new wisdom today the only comes from God. Wisdom is the principle thing and today you have possess that which is primal. Your experiences have all taught you and trained you into the way of righteousness. The fear of the Lord has birthed within you the seed of wisdom. Now you will begin to think, speak, and understand in a new dimension.

I prophesy today that wisdom will have her perfect work in you. I speak over your mind and heart that you possess the mind of Christ, and you make judgments and decisions as He would. May your life begin to reflect a new habit that only wisdom can bring.

James 1:5 - If any of you lack wisdom, let him ask of God, that giveth to all men liberally, and upbraideth not; and it shall be given him.

MAY 31

Today the Lord favors you with His name. His name is wonderful, counselor, mighty God, Prince of Peace, and Everlasting Father. His name bears weight and makes demons tremble. His name is greater than any other. Today you carry that name with you everywhere you go. You possess the name that causes healing to your body and prosperity to your house. You possess the name that saves souls and calms all fears. His name in known in all of heaven and in the lower parts of the earth, You have access and authority to use THAT name... JESUS!

I prophesy today that you go throughout the earth bearing the name of the Lord. I speak that your enemies will flee, cease, and desist when you arrive because you are the bearer of the name of the Lord. You walk with power and authority today. And because you bear His name, He in return makes your name great.

Acts 4:12 - Neither is there salvation in any other: for there is none other name under heaven given among men, whereby we must be saved.

JUNE

"The Month of Humanity"

JUNE 1

Today God sends people into your life to bless you. You will begin to meet people who have been sent by God on assignment to bless you. Your faith in humanity has been tarnished by the encounters of the past. But today God rebuilds your trust in humanity again.

Today I prophesy to you that you are healed from the wounds of the past. I speak that you release the spirit of pride that causes you to refuse the blessings that people have for you due to your suspicion of manipulation. Your mind and heart are healed today that you may receive what is coming to you. God will bless you and those blessings will come through the hands of men.

Luke 6:38 - Give, and it shall be given unto you; good measure, pressed down, and shaken together, and running over, shall men give into your bosom. For with the same measure that ye mete withal it shall be measured to you again.

JUNE 2

Today God send people into your life to witness your gifts and talents. You have been in obscurity and on the backside of the mountain of exposure. But today God begins to reveal you to those who will platform you and give you opportunity. Men will see what the Lord has placed in the inside of you and celebrate the God within you. Your gifts will be seen of men but glorify God.

I prophesy today that you begin to walk through doors and in rooms that your name has been only spoken in. I speak a sharpness and accuracy in your gifts that you are being preferred and called upon by communities that will benefit from what the Lord has given you.

1 Peter 2:12 - Having your conversation honest among the Gentiles: that, whereas they speak against you as evildoers, they may by your good works, which they shall behold, glorify God in the day of visitation.

JUNE 3

Today you will partner with God in every area of your life. Today you will experience the glorious collision of divinity and humanity in full agreement with one another. The entire godhead meets you and brings to pass all that He has promised in your life. Every part of your being is affected by His word and will over your life.

I prophesy to you today that you fully submit to God taking full control and having autonomy over your whole life. All of Him wants all of you today. May you yield to His leading and His promptings. May you walk in the ways of the Lord and your steps be light and your footing be sure. God is within you.

Job 22:21 - Acquaint now thyself with him, and be at peace: thereby good shall come unto thee.

JUNE 4

Today God sends you to the four corners of the earth to be a witness of His goodness and grace. Prepare yourself to travel and encounter new relationships of which you shall be the vehicle of the gospel. People who do not know you will hear your testimony. You will also meet people who God is sending to you that come from the four corners of the earth. You are going to the world and the world will come to you. It will be a divine exchange that occurs when you meet.

I prophesy today that you have the gift of many tongues. You will speak the language of men so that they may hear the message you have to carry to them. I speak over your life that you have a presence that is inviting and engaging, so that others may come to you and hear from you. Be prepared to have global impact and effect. Even the tools of the internet and social media will be a resource to serve you in this season.

Mark 16:15 - And he said unto them, Go ye into all the world, and preach the gospel to every creature.

JUNE 5

Today is the day that you receive grace from your friends and tribe. There has been harshness and cruelty that you have experienced. But today is the day that you will receive grace from your friends. The Lord has dealt with them and has given them a heart for you. They will be moved with compassion towards you, and they will know how to minister to you in this season. Those who do not express this grace towards you are not your tribe.

I prophesy today that you begin to receive as you have given. May your heart be open to accept the love and kindness from those whom God has placed in your path. No longer will you reap a harvest of malice when you have sown the seed of kindness. The grace of God is with you and now you shall see the grace of your friend.

Luke 18:5 - Yet because this widow troubleth me, I will avenge her, lest by her continual coming she weary me.

JUNE 6

Today God puts you in company with people that will contribute to your priorities and purpose. Today you will experience divine partnerships. God has set aside individuals who are assigned to assist you in fulfilling the purpose of God in your life. You will have a revelation of who they are. You will behold their gifts, talents and abilities and understand their purpose in your life.

Today I prophesy that you receive the partners that God has ordained for you. Heaven already backs you up, but also God has placed men in the earth who will also work in agreement with what He has ordained. Today you will make those connections and evil cannot hinder this union.

Nehemiah 4:6 - So built we the wall; and all the wall was joined together unto the half thereof: for the people had a mind to work.

JUNE 7

Today there is a presence of God that comes over you to make you whole. God's desire for you is that you are complete in every way. It is His will for you to be complete in ways that will honor Him. The wounds of your past and of previous experiences have left a void within you that you have hidden away. But today God comes for the voids. He fills them with His presence and makes you complete in Him.

I prophesy today that you begin to expose to the Lord all those things that hurt you, harmed you or cause you to be unsettled. He comes for the truth of your pain, and He makes you whole in every area. Today is the day you are made complete for the assignment that you have been called and the life He has ordained for you to live.

John 5:6 - When Jesus saw him lie, and knew that he had been now a long time in that case, he saith unto him, Wilt thou be made whole?

JUNE 8

Today a new you emerge to the surface. You have been evolving into what God has called you to. The old you has been swallowed up in victory and the you that God has been calling for now comes to pass. You will be new in all your ways. Your desires are new. Your character is made new. Your habits are new. Your perspective is new. All things new for you in this season.

Today I prophesy that you will permit the new you to come forth so that you may experience the blessings that has been in store for you. I speak over you that you will yield to the pulling of the spirit as God places a demand upon the anointing that He has invested within you.

Ezekiel 11:19 - And I will give them one heart, and I will put a new spirit within you; and I will take the stony heart out of their flesh, and will give them an heart of flesh:

JUNE 9

Today is the day that you walk in deliverance from everything that hinders your progress. The chains and hold that bind you are coming off. The things that oppose you are being removed and the things that hold you back are being loosed. God is calling for your deliverance today.

I prophesy a mighty deliverance upon you today. You are called to greater, and you are designed to be further. You will be held back no longer. You are being made free from the grips of stagnation and hindrances. Walk in your deliverance. It is a new day for you.

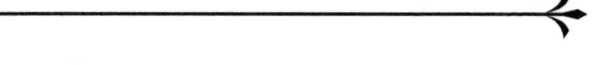

John 8:36 - If the Son therefore shall make you free, ye shall be free indeed.

JUNE 10

Today you will see others favor you by avoiding the regular systems of bureaucracy. God is allowing you to cut through the red tape quickly. Others have been made to endure the systems that are in place, but you will find favor with representatives that will hand lead you through the process quickly. It will be easy for you because God has appointed those who have influence to walk you through it.

Today I prophesy that you embrace the favor that is upon your life. I prophesy that you trust the people that God places in your life that you may see and experience the favorable opportunities they will offer you.

Ruth 2:15-16 - And when she was risen up to glean, Boaz commanded his young men, saying, Let her glean even among the sheaves, and reproach her not: And let fall also some of the handfuls of purpose for her, and leave them, that she may glean them, and rebuke her not.

JUNE 11

Today God reveals to you those who are consistent in your life. God will stabilize you with relationships that are a blessing to you. God will cause you to see how their willingness to remain will serve purpose in endurance for you. The Lord settles you with relationships that are strong and worthy of your future. You will know who they are.

I speak to you prophetically that you walk in a place of peace and understanding concerning all your relationships. May you receive recompense for the things you have sown into others. May God's law of reciprocation come to you, and you are shown no little kindness by those who love you.

Ruth 1:16 - And Ruth said, Intreat me not to leave thee, or to return from following after thee: for whither thou goest, I will go; and where thou lodgest, I will lodge: thy people shall be my people, and thy God my God:

JUNE 12

Today is the day that you partner with God concerning the plans He has for your life. God has a plan that involves you. This plan was in place before you were born. You must fulfill the purpose of God in your life. God has been revealing this plan to you piece by piece. Now you must agree and partner with this plan.

I prophesy today that you are in total agreement with God and His plans for you. May you covenant with God today and make a pact that you will comply with all that He speaks and does in your life. May this covenant be everlasting until the day of Jesus Christ.

Isaiah 14:27 - For the Lord of hosts hath purposed, and who shall disannul it? and his hand is stretched out, and who shall turn it back?

JUNE 13

Today God shows you those in your life that serve as a resource of rebellion against His will. The subtlety of the enemy has caused some to come in to distract you from the original purpose. You must be aware of them and know who they are. God opens your eyes today that you may see. There are those who are contrary to what the Lord has ordered for you. If you are blind to them, you will be taken off track. Open your eyes today.

I prophesy to you today that you have the eye of the eagle, and you are able to see afar off. I speak over you that you have the discernment of a deer and can decipher enemies that are lurking. May you have the boldness of a lion that you may be able to deal with these relationships with courage.

1 Samuel 12:14 - If ye will fear the Lord, and serve him, and obey his voice, and not rebel against the commandment of the Lord, then shall both ye and also the king that reigneth over you continue following the Lord your God:

#GwendasGod

JUNE 14

Today is the day that you will go from overlooked to the preferred. For some time, it has felt as if opportunities have passed you by and you have missed your moment. But today the Lord assures you that your time has not gone by you. You are still in the plan of God and your best days are ahead of you.

I prophesy today that the rooms that you have been awaiting to enter, you are now being invited into. You were once an option but not you are the decided choice of those who have influence and affluence. May your opportunity come and not pass you by. May you be well equipped when it arrives, and you meet it with a prepared heart.

Daniel 6:3 - Then this Daniel was preferred above the presidents and princes, because an excellent spirit was in him; and the king thought to set him over the whole realm.

JUNE 15

Today God gives you rest from the labor you have endured. Your body, your soul and your spirit must rest for what is to come. The season of labor has made you active and busy. But now you must rest because there is another season coming next that will require your full attention and your full strength. God is calling you to rest and prepare. As you do this, you will be fully restored and furnished for what is next.

I prophesy to you today that you obey the signs of rest that your life is calling for. I rebuke exhaustion and burn out. You will not be overwhelmed or frustrated because of the lack of time or energy. God gives you the wisdom of strategy to take the time to rest. You will need it.

Psalms 4:8 - I will both lay me down in peace, and sleep: for thou, Lord, only makest me dwell in safety.

JUNE 16

Today love will come to you in many ways. The people you love and the ones that love you will remind you of the Love of God. God surrounds you with His love today. You will not be without the love that is needed to secure you and your future. You will love again, and you will see that others love you. Particularly, you will be the recipient of love from others.

Today I prophesy the balm of love to cover you and anoint you into healing. Your wounds and scars of the past have made you anxious about new relationships, but the Lord applies the salve of His love to your heart so that you may witness restoration.

Titus 3:4 - But after that the kindness and love of God our Saviour toward man appeared,

JUNE 17

Today placement has its perfect work in your life. God begins to place and position people in order and alignment in your life. The misplacement of relationships, acquaintances and people have misaligned you from your destiny. But God jolts you and them in place today. Do not disregard the tugging and the pulling that He is doing. It is only to align people properly in your life.

I prophesy today that you walk with the wisdom of discernment that you no longer grant people the title they do not deserve nor the positions they haven't been proven to hold in your life. The wisdom of God be with you for this hour of alignment, and may you agree and know that it is God.

1 Chronicles 17:9 - Also I will ordain a place for my people Israel, and will plant them, and they shall dwell in their place, and shall be moved no more; neither shall the children of wickedness waste them any more, as at the beginning,

JUNE 18

Today I speak life over you and all your family. You all will live longer and not die to declare the good works of the Lord. The Lord adds years to your life and cause you to prosper in life. Today you will behold life abundantly. You will experience the life that God intends for you to live. It is a blessed life.

I prophesy today that you welcome this life for you and your family. I rebuke generational curses of disease and sickness that has traveled through your bloodline. I curse predisposed illnesses that cause you to anticipate infirmities. May you receive the word of life that is spoken into you today. May you stand proxy for all your family members that they may come under the auspices of this word.

Psalms 91:16 - With long life will I satisfy him,
and shew him my salvation.

JUNE 19

Today you will see God's judgment upon the heads of those who have come up against you. You have kept silent on matters that were unfavorable for you. You have not repaid the offense that was done to you. But the Lord has seen it and has examined your silence. Now heaven responds for you. You need not fight, because the Lord will be your defense.

I prophesy today that you maintain the heart of God. Rejoice not when you see this judgment executed, but immediately hasten to the altar to pray. The fear of the Lord will keep you in this hour. Today God repays everyone who has dome you harm or wished evil upon you.

Romans 12:19 - Dearly beloved, avenge not yourselves, but rather give place unto wrath: for it is written, Vengeance is mine; I will repay, saith the Lord.

JUNE 20

Today is the day that you see life come full circle for you. People from your past will come to revisit you and you will see restoration unfold for you. A cycle is coming back around to reward you and people who you thought forgot you will come again to bless you. You are not forgotten. The Lord God has caused that which is owed to you to come to you again.

I prophesy to you today that the field of your life is ripe for harvest and the cycle of the last season has been completed. May you now reap the harvest of the last season's labor and your rewards be plenteous.

Genesis 41:14 - Then Pharaoh sent and called Joseph, and they brought him hastily out of the dungeon: and he shaved himself, and changed his raiment, and came in unto Pharaoh.

JUNE 21

Today is the day that God disavows those who volunteer to oppose you. There are evils that follow you, but you are protected by the will and hand of God. The Lord rejects all that rejects you. He blesses all that blesses you. The rejected of the Lord are exposed today and you will not be caught in the snare of their willful wickedness.

I prophesy to you today that you not become contaminated with the nature of those who oppose you. May you never adopt the principles they employ to use strife against others. Keep your heart pure and refrain from the ills of man's evil ways.

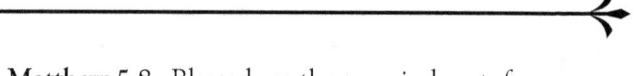

Matthew 5:8 - Blessed are the pure in heart: for they shall see God.

JUNE 22

Today the Lord surrounds you with people who are happy and giving. You have been exposed to the takers, but the givers are coming to sow into you. The Lord sends people who are light in spirit and are pleasant to be around. There is a happiness that surrounds you that will overwhelm you. In this atmosphere the spirit of giving will have liberty because trust is present.

Today I prophesy that you begin to smile and laugh more. Laughter will be your portion and it will cause you to be healed from deep wounded places. May you welcome the relationships that will join in laughter and happiness with you. May a liberal exchange be your portion as you embrace this new season.

Psalms 133:1 - Behold, how good and how pleasant it is for brethren to dwell together in unity!

JUNE 23

Today is the day that you will see the girls and women of your life blessed. You will hear of promotions, increase, healing, and favor coming from their lips. They will testify to you of how God has blessed them. There is a blessing for every female in your life. God shines the light of Hid presence upon them, and the eyes of the Lord turn in their direction.

I prophesy to every woman you know that she will be crowned with the favor of God today. May she increase in every way and her rewards be great. I speak over their wombs that they produce naturally and spiritually all the seeds of purpose and destiny that the Lord has ordained. They will all give birth and bring forth.

Esther 2:17 - And the king loved Esther above all the women, and she obtained grace and favour in his sight more than all the virgins; so that he set the royal crown upon her head, and made her queen instead of Vashti.

JUNE 24

Today the Lord challenges you to change your wardrobe so that you are dressed for what He is calling you to. You must begin to adorn yourself for where you are headed and not where you are. You must be dressed for your future and no longer resemble your past. Change your clothes and begin to obtain a new wardrobe because the Lord is sending you through new doors. You will begin to have an impact and affect the loves of many.

I prophesy to your resources and your increase that it will be made manifested so that you may acquire the things needed for your future. The Lord sets you aside and He dresses you for where you are going. You will not only have the tools for the future, but you will look like it.

Exodus 39:41 - The cloths of service to do service in the holy place, and the holy garments for Aaron the priest, and his sons' garments, to minister in the priest's office.

JUNE 25

Today there is a refinement that comes from trainers and teachers. The Lord sends people in your life that will aide in getting you to the place of purpose. They will sharpen your skills and place a demand upon you for more on a greater level. This is the hour of sharpening for you. The mentors, teachers and trainers are being exposed so that you may submit to their tutelage and heed their instructions.

I prophesy to you today that you will not allow yourself to resist the instructions of the people that God is sending. Do not allow pride or jealousy to cause you to miss the opportunities that are beginning to open for you. Educational and professional training opportunities are opening to you. The Lord has sent it your way.

Proverbs 27:17 - Iron sharpens iron, and one man sharpens another.

JUNE 26

Today your confidence in yourself increases. You will begin to see yourself in the image of God as you were created. No longer will you degrade your appearance or your skill sets. Today you totally embrace who you are and how you appear, and you begin to take pride in your presentation.

I prophesy to you today a healing and wholeness upon you that you may being to see yourself as God sees you. May your eyes begin to perceive yourself in the image of the creator and may you welcome the confidence and assurance that comes along with it. I rebuke low self-esteem and low self-confidence. Be open to seeing who you really are in God.

Psalms 139:14 - I will praise thee; for I am fearfully and wonderfully made: marvellous are thy works; and that my soul knoweth right well.

JUNE 27

Today is the day that you receive the grace and strength to endure your cross. There is a necessary cross that you must bear. You have been appointed for this. God has given you the grace to endure this. You cannot avoid this cross or this season. On the other side of this season is a great resurrection and great power. You cannot receive power without this cross. Bearing this cross will not only release you power, but it will save others.

I prophesy to you today a new strength. This is the strength that only comes from God. Be strong in your mind, your spirit, and your body. May you also have the will to endure. Enduring strength is your portion even today.

Philippians 2:8 - And being found in fashion as a man, he humbled himself, and became obedient unto death, even the death of the cross.

JUNE 28

Today is the day that the earth yields to you her fruit. You will possess the rewards that the earth has to offer, and you will eat of the fat of the land. You have sown yourself, and you will now reap the harvest of those seeds. God will cause the rewards to be great and perfect.

I prophesy to you today that you receive all that God has allowed to come your way. I prophesy to your fields, your barns and your storehouse that it may all be filled with plenty. You will lack nothing in this season for God will send you the blessing of fruitfulness.

Psalms 67:6 - Then shall the earth yield her increase; and God, even our own God, shall bless us.

JUNE 29

Today God causes those around you to change their minds concerning you. You need not chase rumors or lies. The Lord will fight for you. He has seen and heard what has been spoken concerning you. He will defend your name and your reputation. You only need to be silent. For the hour has come when those who spoke against you will come to change their testimony about you. They will apologize and repent.

I prophesy to you today that you remain consistent in your behavior and your will to please the Lord. May your consistency reward you with favorableness. Remain settled in God and do not waiver your testimony or witness. The Lord is with you.

Acts 28:6 - Howbeit they looked when he should have swollen, or fallen down dead suddenly: but after they had looked a great while, and saw no harm come to him, they changed their minds, and said that he was a god.

JUNE 30

Today you grow to a new place of maturity and sacrifice. The Lord has been calling you higher and demanding more from you. This is the day that you respond to His desires. You now begin to see things differently and more maturely. God has done a work in your heart that has changed your perspective and outlook. Now you see them from the standpoint of God.

Today I prophesy that you begin to step into new places of maturity in your mindset and spirit. The way you used to see things and understand them are no more. You have graduated to another place in God. Your faith is increasing, and your sacrifices are becoming great. For this, your anointing has increased.

Luke 22:42 - Saying, Father, if thou be willing, remove this cup from me: nevertheless not my will, but thine, be done.

JULY

"The Month of Completion & Perfection"

JULY 1

Today Gods perfection will be made known to you. You will testify that it was all God who has done a mighty work for you. Gods fullness is being revealed to you. This is a season that you will see the hand of God fully operating on your behalf. It will not be by mans hand, but by the hand of God. He alone will do this for you.

I prophesy to you today that you will embrace all of God and His fullness. You will not miss God in the hour. He will completely come to you to minister to you and fellowship with you. May your heart be open to Him. May your life be effected by Him. May your spirit yield to Him. He is with you now.

1 Peter 3:15 - But sanctify the Lord God in your hearts: and be ready always to give an answer to every man that asketh you a reason of the hope that is in you with meekness and fear:

JULY 2

Today God is completing your testimony by ending your test. The last testing that you have endured has now come to an end. God is ending that season for you. Your testimony has been sealed and is now ready for you to share with others. You've had to hold your peace, but now you can tell what the Lord has done and what He has brought you through.

Today I prophesy to you that you begin to share your witness with others of what the Lord has done. I speak the spirit of boldness upon you to testify. May you prepare yourself to be a witness of what God has done. This season is over for you and you have come through victoriously.

1 John 4:14 - And we have seen and do testify that the Father sent the Son to be the Saviour of the world.

JULY 3

The complete and full Godhead surrounds you today to satisfy your prayer requests. You have petitioned the Lord and your prayers have been heard. The Father, the Son and the Holy Spirit are coming to you to answer you. The Father comes to answer your prayers of need. The Son comes to answer your prayers of desires. The Holy Spirit comes to answer your prayers of wants. You are being satisfied today by the complete Godhead.

I prophesy to you that you are made full from the presence of the Lord. There will no longer be any empty spaces in your life. The Lord God is filling every area of your life. May you begin to exhale from stress and worry as God give you Himself completely.

1 Peter 5:10 - But the God of all grace, who hath called us unto his eternal glory by Christ Jesus, after that ye have suffered a while, make you perfect, stablish, strengthen, settle you.

JULY 4

Today you shall have the perfect motivation to accomplish the tasks you are faced with. God sends a wind to blow behind you that will push you further into your purpose. It will be perfect for you. The timing will be perfect and the movement will be perfect. God has prepared you for this day and now He sends the right wind to push you into it.

I prophesy to you today that you do not resist the wind that is coming to your back which will thrust you into your next. Flow with what is behind you. It is the wind of God for you in this hour. Let it compel you to the vision that God has shown you.

1 Chronicles 14:15 - And it shall be, when thou shalt hear a sound of going in the tops of the mulberry trees, that then thou shalt go out to battle: for God is gone forth before thee to smite the host of the Philistines.

JULY 5

Today you walk in perfect grace. God gives you the space and opportunity to move further towards your dreams. You will know the grace of God completely for this hour. You will behold the strength and knowledge of heaven to walk into a new place. God graces you for this. It is the timing of the Lord for you to move forward.

Today I prophesy to you that you do not slow your feet nor hesitate your moving. God has graced you to move forward. I speak to your feet that all the slothfulness is gone out of them and there is the speed of acceleration in your feet. The grace of God is completely with you for this next move.

2 Corinthians 12:9 - And he said unto me, My grace is sufficient for thee: for my strength is made perfect in weakness. Most gladly therefore will I rather glory in my infirmities, that the power of Christ may rest upon me.

JULY 6

Today God is completing your circle of friends and influencers for this season. Who you need is already with you. No need to search for others because God has already sent you who is needed for where you are going next. God has surrounded you with the right people and the right skills are with them. God is completing your circle of tribe. The people you need are with you now.

I prophesy to you today that you begin to see what the Lord has already blessed you with. I speak to your eyes that they be open to behold the great people who are with you now. May you embrace every relationship with the intention of heaven and may you be fulfilled in your heart because of them.

Philippians 2:25 - Yet I supposed it necessary to send to you Epaphroditus, my brother, and companion in labour, and fellow soldier, but your messenger, and he that ministered to my wants.

JULY 7

Today is the day to be perfectly complete and completely perfect in your dealings. God has graced you today to walk in a realm of perfection. This is not without error, but it is a place of maturity and completion. You are lacking nothing in this hour. You possess what is needed to face the time and the tasks before you.

I prophesy to you today that you maturely face all the tasks as God has sent them to you. I speak over your mind that you begin to elevate your thinking and therefore elevate your behavior. May the grace of perfection and completion follow you throughout the day today.

Colossians 4:12 - Epaphras, who is one of you, a servant of Christ, saluteth you, always labouring fervently for you in prayers, that ye may stand perfect and complete in all the will of God.

JULY 8

Today is the day that God gives you a complete new start on an old dream. There are things that God has given you years ago that you've put off or forgotten about. But today the Lord reminds you of those things and gives you grace to begin again. You will only need to muster up the courage to go back to the drawing board and dare to dream again. This time it will be better and bigger than before.

I prophesy to you today that you begin to dream again. I provoke your dreams to live and I awaked the dreamer in you. I speak over your fears and I command them all to dismantle and disintegrate. This is your hour of a brand new start and it will not be wasted.

Genesis 8:1 - And God remembered Noah, and every living thing, and all the cattle that was with him in the ark: and God made a wind to pass over the earth, and the waters asswaged;

JULY 9

Today God does a complete deliverance within you from the things that has plagued your spirit. You have been seeking breakthrough from those things in your life that has tormented you and the things that you have struggled with. Today the Holy Spirit breaks all covenants that have been made with the things that don't please the Lord. You are being made completely free.

I prophesy to you today that you begin to embrace the freedom that you now walk into. I speak over your spirit that you break all connections, ties and covenants with the things that take you backwards. God is determined to get you to destiny and today is a pivotal point in the right direction.

1 Corinthians 7:21 - Art thou called being a servant? care not for it: but if thou mayest be made free, use it rather.

JULY 10

Today you will possess complete authority over the things God has given under your care. You possess the power to say yes or no. You possess the authority to determine if a thing is alive or dead. You walk in the authority of words, behavior and atmosphere. The Holy Spirit within you will lead and guide you all the way. You need only depend upon Him, for He will show you the way.

I prophesy to you today that you take possession of this God-given authority and you subdue, take dominion and replenish. I speak over your will that it is totally submitted to God to glorify Him. You are in authority, but you are also under authority. Things submit to you to the same level that you submit to God.

Genesis 1:28 - And God blessed them, and God said unto them, Be fruitful, and multiply, and replenish the earth, and subdue it: and have dominion over the fish of the sea, and over the fowl of the air, and over every living thing that moveth upon the earth.

JULY 11

Today is the day that you quit quitting. It is the final day of you giving up on dreams, visions and God-given aspirations. You have often been consistent at being inconsistent. You have left too many things in your life incomplete. But today the Lord is doing a mighty work within you. You are resigning from a life of incompletion. You will finish what you've started and you will end the day, the month, the year and this season successfully.

I prophesy to you today that you are made free from the quitting spirit. May you rid your life of the excuses not to go any further. You are being compelled by the Lord to pick up and move into your purpose. No more quitting.

Matthew 24:13 - But the one who endures to the end will be saved.

JULY 12

Today is the day that you come under the complete divine authority of God. There are things that are out of your control and only the Lord can do this. You will begin to see the Lord take over for you when you are most vulnerable and unsure of what to do. He will fight for you. He will speak for you. He will be your God and He is in control.

Today I prophesy to you that you give total control over to God. I speak to your pride and command it to submit and surrender to the auspices of God. You need not worry or concern yourself with what will be. The Lord will take care of it all. He is in complete control.

Matthew 21:42 - Jesus saith unto them, Did ye never read in the scriptures, The stone which the builders rejected, the same is become the head of the corner: this is the Lord's doing, and it is marvelous in our eyes?

JULY 13

Today is the day that you no longer rebel against the will of God for your life. Our flesh has no desire to please the Lord. It fights against His will. But the more we yield to the Holy Spirit, we will begin to see the rebellious nature of our flesh break. Today you will experience this mighty work in your life. As you obey the commandment of the Lord, you will see your flesh surrender more and more. This will please the Lord.

I prophesy to you today that you walk in total obedience to what God is asking of you in this season. I prophesy over your will that it begins to surrender to God. May you gain the strength that's in discipline to command your flesh to die to its own will but live out the will of God.

1 Samuel 12:14 - If ye will fear the Lord, and serve him, and obey his voice, and not rebel against the commandment of the Lord, then shall both ye and also the king that reigneth over you continue following the Lord your God:

JULY 14

Today you will see the God of protection and safety stand strong in your life. God will guard you from the evils that are in the world. He will keep your body, your mind and your spirit. You will surely dodge that which was designed to harm you. It will not come near you or those you love. You will be protected from the hurt, harm and danger.

I prophesy to you today that you remain under the canopy of this divine protection. May the blood of Jesus cover you in every area of your life. I speak to all that concerns you that it all remains shielded from peril or danger. God will provide safeguard for you in this hour.

Psalms 91:1 - He that dwelleth in the secret place of the most High shall abide under the shadow of the Almighty.

JULY 15

Today is the day that God gives you perfect rest. This is not just the rest of relaxation and rejuvenation, though you will experience that as well, this is the rest of seeing things come together and everyone in place. On the seventh day God rested from creation. This means that He stopped and celebrated what was created. This is what you have come into today, a time of celebration of your work and labor.

I prophesy to you today that you have a Sabbath moment. I speak a grand celebration of all your hard work. May this begin to be a season of rest for you because the work is completed. I speak the right things and the right people are in place so that you do not have to toil as you have done before. Rest.

Genesis 2:2 - And on the seventh day God ended his work which he had made; and he rested on the seventh day from all his work which he had made.

JULY 16

Today is the day that God deals with all your fears by granting you perfect love. Fear has caused you to miss the blessings of the lord and has delayed you from the timing of the lord. But today God gives you a love so perfect that your fears are being dismantled. God has not given you the spirit of fear, but today He gives you love, power and soundness of mind.

Today I prophesy boldness upon you and courage to be with you. You will walk as you have never done so before. I speak to your mind that anxiety has no place there and all phobias are dismissed. You are bold and courageous. You will take on tasks and activities that you once feared with the bravery that God gives you.

1 John 4:18 - There is no fear in love; but perfect love casteth out fear: because fear hath torment. He that feareth is not made perfect in love.

JULY 17

Today you will experience perfect alignment with associations and businesses that will propel you further into your future. There is a mighty work that God has called you to do. It will take partnerships with groups and companies to accomplish this task. God will begin to align you today with these collectives so that the resources you need access to can be granted. This connection will be a divine connection and it will position you for greater.

I prophesy to you today that you begin to flow in the right direction and that you are placed in the right position to come in contact with who you need for what is next. May God begin to shift you into your next even right now. May you agree with the connection and possess the right language to impact the communities you are called to serve.

Luke 1:1 - Forasmuch as many have taken in hand to set forth in order a declaration of those things which are most surely believed among us,

JULY 18

Today you will grab hold of life in a new way. Today you are bound to live a full and complete life. You will begin to embrace a new revelation on living an abundant life, a healthy life, a full life and a life that pleases God. All things that disturb or disrupt your life for reasons of defeat are dismissed. God will begin to pour into you strength and purpose of living that energizes you to go after your dreams.

Today I prophesy to you to live. You will live abundantly and full. There will be no lack in your life. You will be complete in your dealings and full in your goings. I speak over your entire life and I command it to be full and stay filled for the rest of your days.

2 Kings 18:32 - Until I come and take you away to a land like your own land, a land of corn and wine, a land of bread and vineyards, a land of oil olive and of honey, that ye may live, and not die: and hearken not unto Hezekiah, when he persuadeth you, saying, The Lord will deliver us.

JULY 19

Today God gets behind the decrees you've made over your life. Every word that you have spoken and every decision that you have made has been heard from heaven. God is causing your words to come to pass. Heaven is responding to what you have said. You will see things that you have prayed for and spoken in times past begin to manifest in your life. God is coming for your words.

I prophesy to you today that you begin to remember what you have spoken and what you have said. Those words will come back to bless you and cause you to walk in another realm of favor. May your words carry the weight of heaven and may your speech be as a mighty ruler.

Daniel 10:12 - Then said he unto me, Fear not, Daniel: for from the first day that thou didst set thine heart to understand, and to chasten thyself before thy God, thy words were heard, and I am come for thy words.

JULY 20

Today God is releasing reparation to you for the last season of your life. Your season of lack and struggle has been noted in heaven. The things that the enemy has done to you and your family has not only come to an end, but you are now being rewarded by heaven for bearing it all. God is repaying you for the toiling that you endured and sending help according to your confession of faith.

I prophesy to you today that you complete the cycle of suffering and that you enter into the time of redemption. May you receive payment from every entity that caused you harm and may it come to you one thousand fold. It is a time of collection for you and you will not lack for anything.

Ruth 2:12 - The Lord recompense thy work, and a full reward be given thee of the Lord God of Israel, under whose wings thou art come to trust.

JULY 21

Today you are completing a cycle of iniquity in your life. The things that you have done that dishonored God are now being washed out of you. You will no longer desire or crave those things that pull you away from the will of God. Your flesh is being subjected to the will of the Lord.

I prophesy to you today that you begin to die to the old desires and be cleansed from the things that contaminate you. I speak a new will within you that you desire more of God than ever before. You are finished with that old decision and the old life. You are now made new in Christ and you are complete in Him.

John 8:11 - She said, No man, Lord. And Jesus said unto her, Neither do I condemn thee: go, and sin no more.

JULY 22

Today your inner light will shine and there will be no obscurity of it. God is removing all objects that block your brightness. He is ending the demonic eclipse that has hindered your light from shinning before others. You have been in a dark and obscure place, but now you are being brought to light.

I prophesy to you today that you allow your light to shine. I speak to your gifts, talents and abilities that they begin to be offered to God and shared with people that God is glorified. May you begin to shine brightly in the communities that you are called to serve and may God get the glory out of your life.

Isaiah 60:1 - Arise, shine; for thy light is come, and the glory of the Lord is risen upon thee.

JULY 23

Today God is causing you to birth out what he has placed inside you. You have come full term with carrying this vision and now is the time to bring it forth. Your time of carrying is complete and you have successfully gone full term with it. God has helped you and has strengthened you for this assignment.

I prophesy to you today that you begin to deliver the vision in the environment that is conducive to its purpose. I speak over your mind and heart that you are strong and strategic in sharing the vision. I speak over your body that you are fortified as you bring forth what God has place within you.

Luke 2:6 - And while they were there, the time came for her to give birth.

JULY 24

Today is the day where you will begin training and development for the course of the ministry. You will begin this season of preparation for what you are called to do in the ministry of Christ. There are many areas of ministry and you are called to serve. Even the smallest area needs ministry. God is releasing you into the area that you are called and this is the season for your training.

I prophesy to you today that you begin to be led by the Lord as to where you are called to serve in ministry. May you allow the lord to take you through the training and development of that area of ministry. I speak over your heart that it has a fierce desire to work the work of the lord and to serve others.

Galatians 5:13 - For, brethren, ye have been called unto liberty; only use not liberty for an occasion to the flesh, but by love serve one another.

JULY 25

Today complete grace and favor multiplied comes to you. You will see total fulfillment in the things that you do and the grace of God will be completely with you. You have been graced for a work and for things to work for you. The grace that you carry is increased in your life. This is the time of receiving and seeding into what's next for you.

I prophesy to you today that you walk in another level of increase. More than increase of wealth, but increase of favor. I speak over you that you begin to accept what is upon you and with you. The grace if God is not just with you but also with you in an amplified way.

2 Peter 1:2 - Grace and peace be multiplied unto you through the knowledge of God, and of Jesus our Lord,

JULY 26

Today the perfection of God will be shown to you through abnormal places and things. God has a plan and He has a way that is far greater than what anyone can think or imagine. God is revealing to you a perfect plan and it will come to you in an unconventional way. Open your eyes today, because God will use things that you are not used to, to speak to you and it will be a perfect expression of God.

I prophesy to you today that you have the ability to see the things that you have once missed. I speak to your ability to hear and receive what God has for you. May you have the grace to behold the perfection of God in ways that you have never known before.

Isaiah 55:8 - For my thoughts are not your thoughts, neither are your ways my ways, saith the Lord.

JULY 27

Today is the day that the hearts of those you have prayed for will surrender to the Lord. You will see the prayers you prayed for others begin to come to pass. Even the prayers you've prayed for yourself will begin to manifest today. God has heard you and He is answering you. It is a good day to contact those in whom you've prayed for salvation and remind them of His goodness. Their heart has been made tender before God. The seed of faith will be watered.

I prophesy to you today that every prayer will begin to receive answers. I speak the results of heaven to come into your life. I speak the seed of your intercession will yield fruits of healing, favor, protection, grace and miracles. May God visit you as you call upon Him in prayer.

Romans 1:9 - For God is my witness, whom I serve with my spirit in the gospel of his Son, that without ceasing I make mention of you always in my prayers;

JULY 28

Today God is favoring you with manifested blessings. This is the season of manifested miracles. You will begin to see, hear, walk in and possess the tangible things you have desired and prayed for. God is perfectly causing the earth to release to you your answers. There is even a blessing concerning real estate and residence. Your living conditions are being blessed and favored by God. Property is being released in the areas that are needed.

I prophesy to you today that you begin to receive what God is releasing into your life. I speak that you will have an open heart to the presence of the Lord and an open hand to His provision and blessing. May you welcome in the new things that He has sent and may you possess the blessing of His provision.

Matthew 19:29 - And every one that hath forsaken houses, or brethren, or sisters, or father, or mother, or wife, or children, or lands, for my name's sake, shall receive an hundredfold, and shall inherit everlasting life.

JULY 29

Today you are completing the cycle of transformation for your future. The Lord has been working on your character, your mindset and your heart in order to bring you to a future that He has promised. You have been evolving into a new person. Today God in completing that change and a new person is arising within you. It is what the Lord has been demanding of you to become. Get ready for the new you to arise.

I prophesy to you today that you begin to welcome the change that has taken place in you. The healing you've been longing for and the breakthrough that you have requested has finally come and you are what your future needs. Accept the change and welcome the newness that comes along with it.

2 Corinthians 3:18 - But we all, with open face beholding as in a glass the glory of the Lord, are changed into the same image from glory to glory, even as by the Spirit of the Lord.

JULY 30

Today you will walk in a new level of wisdom. Your life experiences have yielded a divine knowledge that causes you to become wiser. You are becoming even more mature in your gifts, your perceptions and your outlook on life. The Lord has dealt favorably with you concerning this season and you will properly know how to approach it. You are being favored with the wisdom of the Lord.

Today I prophesy to you that you begin to use the wisdom of God to make sound decisions and right judgments. I speak a new level of soberness to be upon you that causes you to be sought after of men to know what to do in their season. Wisdom will have her perfect work in you.

Daniel 2:23 - I thank thee, and praise thee, O thou God of my fathers, who hast given me wisdom and might, and hast made known unto me now what we desired of thee: for thou hast now made known unto us the king's matter.

JULY 31

Today you will experience the power within the name of Jesus. The authority of His name is with you and causing the things that He desires to be released into your life. His name is causing divine protection to stand tall and firm before you and the enemy cannot infiltrate. The name of the Lord is with you for the days to come. You will possess the power that only His name brings.

I prophesy to you today that you are not afraid to use the name of Jesus wherever you go. May you take authority over every unfavorable situation and turn it to good by utilizing the name of Jesus. I speak a boldness and confidence that only His name can bring upon you now.

Psalms 20:7 - Some trust in chariots, and some in horses: but we will remember the name of the Lord our God.

AUGUST

The Month of New Beginnings

AUGUST 1

Today you will have a new experience and a new beginning with God. God gives you a new start today and allows you to have a do over from the things you've once attempted. This is your new day of new beginnings. The lord will open your eyes to new opportunities and new doors that are about to open. You will have a chance to walk into new places and be graced with new connections. All things new in this season.

I prophesy to you today that the Lord will even deal with you in a new way. He will speak to you in ways that you have never heard Him. He will minister to your soul in ways you have never felt Him. I speak newness in God over you and in you today. May you see and behold NEW!

Ephesians 4:24 - And that ye put on the new man, which after God is created in righteousness and true holiness.

AUGUST 2

Today God will partner you with new people that will walk through new doors with you. You will begin to have new life experiences and it will be with individuals who are as well, on a journey of newness. These new relationships will yield great fruit for many years to come. Open your heart to the new connections because they will announce to you that you are in a new place.

I prophesy to you today new connections and new networks of connections that will serve as resources of support. I speak to the nations and command them to release the people that are assigned by God to connect to you. May your trust issues die at this very moment so that you aren't reluctant to receive the people the Lord has prepared for your future.

Acts 10:28 - And he said unto them, Ye know how that it is an unlawful thing for a man that is a Jew to keep company, or come unto one of another nation; but God hath shewed me that I should not call any man common or unclean.

AUGUST 3

Today God will refresh you in every area. God will touch you in a very whole way. He is touching your body and renewing your strength and making you new. He is touching your mind, and renewing your thoughts and perception. He is touching your spirit and causing you to have new experiences with Him. This is your day of being totally renewed in God and by God.

I prophesy to you today that you embrace the newness that is occurring within you. I speak a new you to arise out of the ashes of your past. I speak a new you to come forth from the incarceration of yesterday. I speak a new you to spring forth from the bondage that the enemy has set before you. You are made new in every way.

2 Corinthians 5:17 - Therefore if any man be in Christ, he is a new creature: old things are passed away; behold, all things are become new.

AUGUST 4

Today new winds blow in your direction, which will push you further into your purpose. God sends a wind like you've never known which causes you to experience new direction and favor. God commands the new winds to blow behind you to push you. He commands the new winds to blow around you to protect you. He commands the new winds to blow on each side of you to keep you. The new winds of God are blowing in your life today.

I prophesy that you agree with the move of God that is happening. I speak to your feet that they flow with the new wind of God that comes into your life. I speak to your will that it aligns with the word of this prophecy. May you float and flow with what God is doing with you in this season. It is new.

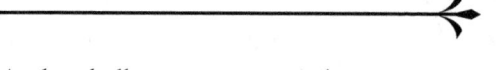

Joel 3:18 - And it shall come to pass in that day, that the mountains shall drop down new wine, and the hills shall flow with milk, and all the rivers of Judah shall flow with waters, and a fountain shall come forth of the house of the Lord, and shall water the valley of Shittim.

AUGUST 5

Today you will behold new grace. God is gracing you in a new way. The grace of God that is upon you has brought you to this present day. Now there is a new grace that rests upon you for a greater work. This is the season to embrace the new grace. The unmerited favor of God is with you to do great things. You're being graced to walk in a new place and take possession of the things that the Lord has ordered for your life. It is a new grace and it is now.

I prophesy to you today that you walk in this grace for this season of your life. You will need this grace in order to accomplish what God has assigned for you. The grace is for now. I speak to your future and command it to come to your present that you may fully understand what is the mind and will of God for your life. May you walk with a new grace.

1 Kings 11:29 - And it came to pass at that time when Jeroboam went out of Jerusalem, that the prophet Ahijah the Shilonite found him in the way; and he had clad himself with a new garment; and they two were alone in the field:

AUGUST 6

Today a new you comes forth. God has been calling for a new you and today is the day you yield to the Holy Spirit. You shall be a new person in every way. Your family and friends will ask you what has changed about you. It is the hand of God pulling you out of the past into your future. You are beginning to look like the future God has planned for you. The new you is coming forth.

I prophesy to you today that you permit this new thing to happen to you. I speak that there is a complete surrender to the will of God. May you yield to the great work of the Holy Spirit. May you give Him a YES to all that He desires for you. I prophesy to you that you become completely NEW!

Isaiah 43:18 - Remember ye not the former things, neither consider the things of old.

AUGUST 7

Today you are completing a cycle in your life and you will go to a new level. Today is your day of promotion. You will graduate to another place in the spirit. Your prayer life and personal devotion with God will be increased. God is sending you to the next level. This is evident that you have successfully completed the last level you were on and you've now become overqualified for this present place. A new place is prepared for you.

I prophesy to you today that you begin to walk out of the completed place and into the new place. You can't remain where you are, you must move on to the next place. I speak promotion and increase upon you until you are too large to hold an old seat. You must move forward to experience comfort and peace.

1 Samuel 18:2 - And Saul took him that day, and would let him go no more home to his father's house.

AUGUST 8

Today is a day of double portion for you. You will see the hand of God release blessings, miracles and provision in twofold ways. Your new is becoming more new. God is strengthening the things He has spoken concerning you. All the things that you are still getting used to that are new, look up because its becoming new again. There is a shift in the atmosphere for you and its newer than before.

I prophesy to you today that you are aware of all stagnation and complacencies in your life. May you now become more and more desirous of newer things. Your appetite is changing for the taste of the new. I speak to your mind that it is sharper and you increasingly think on new ideas, concepts and witty inventions.

Isaiah 61:7 - For your shame ye shall have double; and for confusion they shall rejoice in their portion: therefore in their land they shall possess the double: everlasting joy shall be unto them.

AUGUST 9

Today you are beholding a new deliverance that you have never experienced before. There are things that have held you back and have been a flaw in your progression. God desires to begin to deal with those things today. Deliverance will come in a new way. The areas that you've been avoiding will not change with old measures. It will be a new approach and a new method that will lead you to your freedom.

I prophesy to you today that you begin to embrace the new methods that the lord employs to get you to arrive to your place of promise. No longer look to old methods to gain the progress you desire. It is new and it will cause your dreams to manifest fully. May you say "YES" to this season of breakthrough and healing.

Romans 7:6 - But now we are delivered from the law, that being dead wherein we were held; that we should serve in newness of spirit, and not in the oldness of the letter.

AUGUST 10

Today you are establishing a new order for your life. The order of God is being imposed on your life. You will begin to make changes and adjustments that will reflect this new government. God is determined to catapult you into purpose, but the structure of your life must be right. Things are shifting in a new way. The government of your life is receiving new a foundation. This will be necessary for your next season.

I prophesy to you today that you obtain a God ordained, re-established order in your life. May your ground shift and may your mind be transformed into new. I speak over your life that this shift will align you with your future and your tomorrows will be greater than your yesterdays.

Proverbs 4:18 - But the path of the just is as the shining light, that shineth more and more unto the perfect day.

AUGUST 11

Today there is a new resistance rising in you. A resistance to the things that hold you back from purpose. You have been passive concerning the things that are sensitive and dear to you. However, there is an aggression that is coming out of you. It will cause you to fight back instead of simply allow the enemy to prevail. You will begin to rebel against everything that you have once agreed with which is contrary to your destiny. God gives you strength to do this in this hour.

I prophesy to you today that you begin to increase your faith fight. May you war with the enemies within. May you fight until your will bends to the will of God. I speak strength over you and within you.

Luke 21:15 - For I will give you a mouth and wisdom, which all your adversaries shall not be able to gainsay nor resist.

AUGUST 12

Today is the day that God will establish His new order in your life. Wealth will come to you from many directions. The Lord is instituting His covenant with you in the earth. Things that were in disarray are now being settled through a new way. God has released His word over you and you are earmarked to prosper. No other order will do. The will of the Father prevails above all other orders.

Today I prophetically speak over you that you will walk in this new covenant with God. It is a covenant of wealth and prosperity. May this order release what heaven has declared concerning you. May you behold the fullness of this covenant and submit to the power of this order.

Deuteronomy 8:18 - But thou shalt remember the Lord thy God: for it is he that giveth thee power to get wealth, that he may establish his covenant which he sware unto thy fathers, as it is this day.

AUGUST 13

Today the heart of God will overwhelm your heart. Your heart is being transformed and molded into a new heart. God makes your heart more and more like His. Your eyes will see differently, your ears will hear differently, your mind will think differently and even your feet walk into a new path. The heart of your Heavenly Father now lives in you.

I prophesy to you today that you allow the heart of God to transform you in every way. All the things you have noticed about yourself and all that concerns you is now surrendered to your new heart. May you possess this newness and submit to all it touches and affects. You have the heart of God.

1 Corinthians 14:25 - And thus are the secrets of his heart made manifest; and so falling down on his face he will worship God, and report that God is in you of a truth.

AUGUST 14

Today you will experience a new deliverance. The Lord will bring you out of an old thing in a new way. Your coming out will be unconventional. Your coming forth will be brand new. The Lord will use the strategies of heaven to deliver you into your purpose and your destiny. Prepare yourself today for a great reckoning. It will be miraculous how you will escape the snare that was set for you. But the Lord will cause you to escape.

I prophesy to you today that you willingly follow the instructions and strategies of God. They will yield to you great victories and produce the fruit of your prayers. No matter how uncommon it is, the way of the Lord will provide you the life you have been looking for.

1 Corinthians 5:7 - Purge out therefore the old leaven, that ye may be a new lump, as ye are unleavened. For even Christ our passover is sacrificed for us:

AUGUST 15

Today the Lord will release you into new levels of peace and rest. No matter the toiling you have done, no matter the fights you've been in, you are about to experience rest. You will abandon the old warfare between your flesh and other enemies. Gods will will prevail today and you'll see it manifest.

Today I prophesy to you that you begin to embrace the rest that is being provided for you. I speak over your mind and your body that they both will yield to this call to rest and retreat. This season is the fruit of your labor and rest is now your portion. You will need it for the next season, which will require your full attention.

Ephesians 2:15 - Having abolished in his flesh the enmity, even the law of commandments contained in ordinances; for to make in himself of twain one new man, so making peace;

AUGUST 16

Today the Lord reveals to you a new love that you have never experienced. Not only does the love of God surround you, but you will also understand God's love for you in new ways. In addition, God will send others to love you the way you deserve and desire love. It will be new and it will be refreshing. The Lord has examined you and will answer your prayers.

I prophesy to you today that you open your heart to love. The fullness of God's love is being expressed towards you in many ways. You will receive all the lovely things that God has planned for your life. Today I speak over your life that it will be loved and offer love to others in a very new way.

John 13:34 - A new commandment I give unto you, That ye love one another; as I have loved you, that ye also love one another.

AUGUST 17

Today the Lord brings your life into a new alignment with what He has planned for you. You are not just being re-aligned, but there are new arrangements that you are being molded for. God will cause that which is confusing to be dismantled and he will bring you into perfect agreement with His will for you. When others refuse you, God will set you up with those who will receive you.

Today I prophesy to you that you begin to see with your eyes the other options that God is making available. I speak that you are no longer blinded to what God is doing now. He is making new ways for you. All you must do is come in complete agreement with it.

Isaiah 48:6 - Thou hast heard, see all this; and will not ye declare it? I have shewed thee new things from this time, even hidden things, and thou didst not know them.

AUGUST 18

Today the Lord gives you a new zeal for life and to LIVE! Your life has been filled with disappointments, let downs and displeasure. But today the Lord will begin to change your viewpoint and you will see life and living as you have never before. Your desire to live an abundant life is increasing more and more. You are bound to live.

I prophesy to you today that you open your eyes to see your life as a blessing and not a curse. May you begin to perceive every situation as an opportunity to share the greatness of God within you. I speak over your mind, that it transforms it's discernment of the total you so that you may begin to see yourself as God sees you.

2 Corinthians 3:6 - Who also hath made us able ministers of the new testament; not of the letter, but of the spirit: for the letter killeth, but the spirit giveth life.

AUGUST 19

Today God makes new decisions concerning you. He also makes available new choices that will benefit your future. There are new pathways that you must take and new roads you must trod. The Lord is opening those paths so that you may begin to journey in what He has desired for you. Because of your commitment to Him, He will do this thing for you today.

Today I prophesy to you that you begin to receive what the Lord has decided for you. His choices are better than our choices. May you trust His plan and receive His will. He has already decided for you and He has commanded heaven to agree.

Hebrews 10:20 - By a new and living way, which he hath consecrated for us, through the veil, that is to say, his flesh;

AUGUST 20

Today the Lord causes you to complete another level and begin new levels in Him. You have been toiling through this last dimension, but now you have finished what was required of you. Now you shall embark upon new concentrations that will yield great rewards for you.

I prophesy to you today that you complete every task, assignment and reach every goal you have planned. For now is the time to begin new assignments and tasks. The Lord will give you the strength and the fortitude to complete this level as you have done others.

Acts 20:24 - But none of these things move me, neither count I my life dear unto myself, so that I might finish my course with joy, and the ministry, which I have received of the Lord Jesus, to testify the gospel of the grace of God.

AUGUST 21

Today the Lord births a new will within you. This new will forces the old will to be broken. Your previous resolve is not fit for what the Lord has for you next. You must have a new will. The old will is an enemy to the next season of your life. That nature is being destroyed so that the new nature within you can live to serve and please the Lord the more.

Today I prophesy to you that you allow the new will within you to come forth. I speak over your fears and command them to be powerless. I declare the law of God to have preeminence in your life and over your mind. May you accept what the lord is doing now within you and for you.

Ezekiel 36:26 - A new heart also will I give you, and a new spirit will I put within you: and I will take away the stony heart out of your flesh, and I will give you an heart of flesh.

AUGUST 22

Today the Lord causes a new light to shine within you. The pressures of life and the burdens of purpose have dimmed your light. But today the Lord produces new light within you. Your light will shine for others to see the hope that lies within you. This light will be attractive and cause divine favor to come your way. Be prepared to be blessed.

I prophesy to you today that you allow your new light to shine from within you. God is refining you and sharpening you so that others may inquire. I speak over every dark dimmer that attempts to put out your light that it is powerless. May your light shine brighter and brighter each day.

1 John 2:8 - Again, a new commandment I write unto you, which thing is true in him and in you: because the darkness is past, and the true light now shineth.

AUGUST 23

Today the Lord gives you new spaces to operate in. These spaces will allow your full creativity to come forth and you will see all that lies within you. There will be a birthing of great talents from with you as you welcome these new spaces of creativity. The Lord has caused doors to open and veils to come down so that you may enter into new realms of performance.

I prophesy to you today that you begin to tap into new arenas of opportunity, which will show forth the great things God has placed with you. You have the innate ability like God to create and make good things. You will have the room, space and place to do it now with His peace.

Isaiah 65:17 - For, behold, I create new heavens and a new earth: and the former shall not be remembered, nor come into mind.

AUGUST 24

Today the Lord releases to you the course of ministry and process you must endure. There are holy assignments that God requires you to fulfill. Your hands have ben blessed and graced to do this work. You must not avoid it but you must embrace it. There are Holy orders that you must follow. Today is the day that the Lord reveals to you the work of your hands in His Kingdom.

I prophesy to you today that you put your hands to the plow of the Lord and do not look back. I speak over your life, that it is consecrated for Gods purpose and use. You will walk in the fullness of your divine purpose and you will know what is assigned to your hands.

Luke 1:8-9 - And it came to pass, that while he executed the priest's office before God in the order of his course, According to the custom of the priest's office, his lot was to burn incense when he went into the temple of the Lord.

AUGUST 25

Today you experience new mercies and new favor. New favor from the Lord finds you this day. There are things that were supposed to occur for you in times past. The enemy of your future has held them up. But today you will begin to see a release of this favor upon your life. This is not the old favor this is new favor. It is new because of the new things the Lord will have you do in this hour of your life.

Today I prophesy over your life that it is smeared with new favor. May you walk through this day seasoned with the favor of God for this next season of your life. I speak to streams of blessings and I command them to flow in your direction even now.

Luke 1:30 - And the angel said unto her, Fear not, Mary: for thou hast found favour with God.

AUGUST 26

Today the Lord causes His likeness to come through you. You will no longer have a crisis in identity. You will see Gods reflection within you. You will clearly know who you are and your purpose in this life. The Lord reveals himself within you. This will seem to be a new you, but it has been God within you all the time.

I speak prophetically that you begin to allow God to arise within you. Do not resist the change you are going through. It is a new thing and it comes forth now. May your new identity come forth so that men may know whose you are. Your God-likeness begins to shine forth today.

Colossians 3:10 - And have put on the new man, which is renewed in knowledge after the image of him that created him:

AUGUST 27

Today the Lord releases a new word over your life, which will save your life. The word is "SALVATION"! His saving grace prevails over the will of the enemy to destroy you. But this word does not just save your soul, it also saves your life, your family, your business, your career and everything that concerns you. It all comes under the canopy of this word, SALVATION!

I speak the word of the Lord over you and may it resound over and over. May this word reverberate through your spirit and every area of your being. May all that concerns you submit to this word of deliverance and rescue you from all harm.

SALVATION - SALVATION - SALVATION!!!

Psalms 118:25 - Save now, I beseech thee, O Lord: O Lord, I beseech thee, send now prosperity.

AUGUST 28

Today the Lord births within you a new desire for excellence. Mediocrity and normality will not be able to stand in this next season of your life. There is a very strong craving within you to walk with an excellent spirit. You will stand out above the rest and you will be known for your attention to detail. This is all insight from God. He will sharpen your skills and make strong your ability to produce on another level.

I prophesy to you today that you endure this sharpening season. It is iron that sharpens iron. May you survive the cutting away of the dullness of life and welcome the acuity in knowledge and skill. This will greatly reward you and yield to you bountiful fruits of success.

Proverbs 17:27 - He that hath knowledge spareth his words: and a man of understanding is of an excellent spirit.

AUGUST 29

There is a new change that is coming upon you and it comes from the Lord. Welcome the new changes that are taking place. There is even a change in the company you keep. For when you have changed, then will the people around you follow. The lord provokes this adjustment so that you may meet withal the responsibilities given to you. This is the hour of divine transformation. Embrace it now!

Today I prophesy to you that you will be transformed into another man/woman. You will begin to walk in the fullness of your purpose, but this will require making adjustments. Do not fear the changes that are being made by heaven, but walk in them with confidence and assurance. This is the Lords doing.

Romans 12:2 - And be not conformed to this world: but be ye transformed by the renewing of your mind, that ye may prove what is that good, and acceptable, and perfect, will of God.

AUGUST 30

Today the Lord is calling you to new levels of maturity and consecration. There are minuscule things that have come to distract you and detour you from the will of God. Your new stride for maturity will win the battle over these disruptions. As you commit your mind and your ways to the lord for purification, you will also experience great joy and peace. The contaminants of yesterday will no longer be able to taint your future.

I prophesy to you today that as you consecrate yourself before God, you will begin to experience supernatural growth in your character and mind. There will be an insightful outlook that you will possess which will make you sought after for the wisdom that lies within you. Be prepared to be used of God on new levels.

1 Thessalonians 5:23 - And the very God of peace sanctify you wholly; and I pray God your whole spirit and soul and body be preserved blameless unto the coming of our Lord Jesus Christ.

AUGUST 31

Today you will begin to know God as you have never known Him before. Today the Lord begins to reveal to you His new name. For it is not new to God, but it will be new to you. You have seen Him and known Him in many ways, but there is a new way that He will reveal Himself to you. You will know Him as you have never before.

I prophesy to you today that you open your eyes, your ears and your heart, that you may experience God in a new way. So that He may introduce Himself to you in a new way. May this revelation be life changing for you. May you go and testify of Him who has revealed Himself to you so that others may also know Him. May you know Him and make Him known.

Philippians 3:10 - That I may know him, and the power of his resurrection, and the fellowship of his sufferings, being made conformable unto his death;

SEPTEMBER

"The Month of Bringing Forth"

SEPTEMBER 1

Today you will show God within you. God who is great and mighty, desires that you display His glory to men. He will rise up through you in great ways. Your life will be a testimony of His power and strength. Today you will comfortably yield to allowing the Lord to use you in great ways. Fear or anxiety will not cripple you from showing all that God has placed within you.

I prophesy to you today that you begin to walk in boldness and confidence to allow God to use you. He will glorify Himself through your life. You will begin to allow Him to speak through you, live through you and use you mightily. Each demonstration of His presence will bring you closer to fulfilling your purpose in life.

1 John 4:4 - Ye are of God, little children, and have overcome them: because greater is he that is in you, than he that is in the world.

SEPTEMBER 2

Today you will begin to witness deliverance from the things that hold you back. Today is your day of breakthrough from former things that gripped you. You have been toiling to gain freedom from the things that you war with, within you. But your breaking has come! Receive total freedom from the bondage of the past.

I prophesy to you today that you have the boldness to break free from those things that have plagued you. It can sometimes be difficult to release the things you have grown accustomed to, but today you make the strong decision to let it all go. I speak the strength to walk away from it all and to walk in newness of life.

Acts 16:26 - And suddenly there was a great earthquake, so that the foundations of the prison were shaken: and immediately all the doors were opened, and every one's bands were loosed.

SEPTEMBER 3

Today the fullness of the godhead comes to your rescue to deliver you from you. Oftentimes our war can be externally. However, the war within us is far more detrimental. It is not always the 'enemy', but at times it is the 'inner me' that plagues us. Today God is setting you free from your own decisions and perceptions that have caused you to be held back from your destinies.

I prophesy that you begin to see the areas that are harmful to you and allow the Lord God to sever the ties with those things that are not necessary for your future. I speak a will within you that will rise up and say no more. No more, will you allow you to be the hindrance to yourself. You are being made free right now!

John 8:36 - If the Son therefore shall make you
free, ye shall be free indeed.

SEPTEMBER 4

Today God delivers you from surroundings and environments that are harmful to your future. People and places that are a direct contradiction to what you are assigned to, have surrounded you. But today you are being made free from those places and people. Today is your day of liberation.

I prophesy to you, that you begin to boldly walk away from and depart out of the people and relationships that are going in a different direction from you. You are designed to do a great work in the earth. Environments are crucial and I command you to possess the discernment to know what is good for you and harmful to you.

Jeremiah 34:10 - Now when all the princes, and all the people, which had entered into the covenant, heard that every one should let his manservant, and every one his maidservant, go free, that none should serve themselves of them any more, then they obeyed, and let them go.

SEPTEMBER 5

Today is the day that you breakthrough into grace and favor. Regardless of what has occurred in your life before now, today is the day that you begin to experience favor that is uncommon. Heaven smiles upon you today to bring into your life the things that are beyond your deserving. God makes a decision to bless you today.

I prophesy to you, that you begin to experience this breakthrough in every area of your life. Your finances, your faith, and your future are all effected by the favor of God. You will not lack any good thing in your life. This breaking has been awaiting this time and it has now come for you.

Psalms 84:11 - For the Lord God is a sun and shield: the Lord will give grace and glory: no good thing will he withhold from them that walk uprightly.

SEPTEMBER 6

Today you will receive a breakthrough in your identity. The things you have been asking the Lord to reveal to you about your identity and your purpose will be known today. You will receive a revelation concerning all that is within you and why the Lord put you on this earth. Don't think it strange that the things you see are somewhat regular to you. It is what you really have known all along.

Today I prophesy that you open your eyes, your ears and your heart to what the Lord will show you about yourself. I speak over your mind that it will not delay in receiving all the Lord is saying. May you welcome this identity from the Lord, for it is the true identity to who you are and have always been.

1 Peter 2:9 - But ye are a elect race, a royal priesthood, a holy nation, a people for God's own possession, that ye may show forth the excellencies of him who called you out of darkness into his marvellous light:

SEPTEMBER 7

Today is the day that you complete a cycle in your process of development. You will breakthrough into a new dimension of purpose today. The process has been tedious, but you have endured and now you come to a new plateau. You have arrived to another place in the fullness of your process.

I speak over you today, that you begin to walk in the newness of life. May you begin to speak, see and dwell on this new level. May you welcome all that this level of living has to offer. You will begin to see all that has been awaiting you is on this level. God will direct you as He has done in times past and you will not fail but recover all that is for you.

Romans 6:4 - Therefore we are buried with him
by baptism into death: that like as Christ was
raised up from the dead by the glory of the Father,
even so we also should walk in newness of life.

SEPTEMBER 8

Now that you have completed a cycle, you will begin to breakthrough into new areas of your life. You will walk through new doors. You will have new opportunities. You will even develop new relationships with new people. This is a new time in your life and newness is springing forth for you.

I prophesy to you today, that every obstacle that was in place hindering this newness to be removed NOW, in Jesus' Name! I speak to every blockage and command a divine release that causes the floodgates of heaven to pour out in your life. There will be no area untouched by this new breakthrough that you are experiencing.

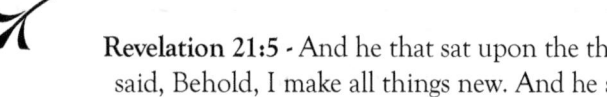

Revelation 21:5 - And he that sat upon the throne said, Behold, I make all things new. And he said unto me, Write: for these words are true and faithful.

SEPTEMBER 9

Today your breakthrough is within you and you will bring it forth. All the things you have been searching for are the things that the Lord has placed on the inside of you. You have what it takes to become what you are supposed to be. You are full of purpose and destiny. All things good and perfect are within you. Now is the time to bring it out. Today is the day to actualize it.

I prophesy to you today, that you begin to pull out the gifts, talents and abilities that are within you. May you begin to operate in the calling that you are divinely called to. I speak to your potential and command it to come forth. As you give birth to it, you will know and understand why you had to survive the previous season of your life.

Leviticus 26:10 - And ye shall eat old store, and bring forth the old because of the new.

SEPTEMBER 10

Today you will receive breakthrough from the arduous process that you have been exposed to. God is speaking to systems of the earth on your behalf and causing them to yield you increase and victory. The Lord is turning the heart of the king in your favor and causing you to receive blessings in an expedited manner.

I prophesy to you today, that you begin to accelerate your movements and move your feet quickly. The Lord is causing a speed to your blessings, to flow towards you quickly. Your next miracle will be a quick work of the Lord.

Amos 9:13-15 - Yes indeed, it won't be long now." God's Decree. "Things are going to happen so fast your head will swim, one thing fast on the heels of the other. You won't be able to keep up. Everything will be happening at once—and everywhere you look, blessings! Blessings like wine pouring off the mountains and hills. I'll make everything right again for my people Israel:

SEPTEMBER 11

Today is the day you receive breakthrough in the stubborn areas of your life. There are some things that you have easily come over and through. But there are other areas that have presented with great resistance. You have toiled with these things for some time now. But today is the day that the stubborn thing is broken and it looses it's strength.

I prophesy to you today, that the might of the obstacle looses its power. May you walk in liberty and freedom from the thing that has resisted you and opposed you. I speak over your levels of endurance and I command them to increase. You are closer to your deliverance than you realize. Today the stubborn thing is removed.

Matthew 12:29 - Or else how can one enter into a strong man's house, and spoil his goods, except he first bind the strong man? and then he will spoil his house.

SEPTEMBER 12

Today you will begin to walk in apostolic power. As the early apostles did, so will you do. You will begin to have demonstration in the spirit of the things of God. You will not have to be an apostle, but the same power that raised up Christ from the dead and that the apostolic fathers walked in is with you also.

I prophesy to you today, that you tap into a new realm of authority and demonstration. This authority is not for you to boast or brag, but rather for you to show forth the glory of God. God's desire to use you is ever increasing and today is a good day to yield to the Holy Spirit. As you do so, you will see things transform in the lives of the people you come in contact with.

Mark 16:17 - And these signs shall follow them that believe; In my name shall they cast out devils; they shall speak with new tongues;

SEPTEMBER 13

Today is the last day you tell the Lord no to the things He has been asking and requiring of you. There has been an heir of rebellion rising in you to all the things you are destined to do. Your resistance to obey it has delayed you in purpose. But no longer will that be. You will say yes to the Lord.

I prophesy to you today, that there is a yes within you that rises. I speak to your will and your emotions that they align with your reason for existence. May you walk and live in agreement with the totality of your purpose, that you surrender your will to its bidding. Break through the rebellion of resistance and come to the place of fulfillment.

Acts 9:6 - And he trembling and astonished said, Lord, what wilt thou have me to do? And the Lord said unto him, Arise, and go into the city, and it shall be told thee what thou must do.

SEPTEMBER 14

Today is the day that you will breakthrough to Passover. You will discover the reason for your deliverance and why you had to endure a hard season. You are not meant to be free for naught. There is a purpose behind this liberty. And it is to get to the other side of life. There is another side of life that you are about to be introduced to. Be prepared to experience another perspective of easy living.

Today I prophesy to you, that you will begin to break out of the places that held you back. And I speak to your feet that you do not stop once you break through. I command you to keep pressing until you Passover to the other side of every situation that seems like the past. May you not be stuck or stagnant in any place. May you keep moving until you get to the other side.

Genesis 31:21 - So he fled with all that he had; and he rose up, and passed over the river, and set his face toward the mount Gilead.

SEPTEMBER 15

Today is the day that you advance into the rest of God. There has been a demonic agenda against you to wear you out and exhaust you before purpose. But the Lord has seen this attempt and has waged war against it. So therefore, God is releasing advancement into His rest for you. You will not be faint or fatigued, but restful for the journey that is before you.

I prophesy to you today, that you take advantage of every moment to rest and be rejuvenated in the Lord. May you exercise wisdom to retreat and steal away so that you might be restored. Be aware of your levels of frustration, for they will reveal the subliminal attack against you. But you will win as you rest your body, your soul and your spirit. You will be made whole as you rest.

Psalms 94:13 - That thou mayest give him rest from the days of adversity, until the pit be digged for the wicked.

SEPTEMBER 16

Today is the day to express the Love of God to all in whom you come in contact with. God is commanding you to show His love to everyone. His desire for you is to express His love in every way to everyone. The Lord has shown you His love and now He is compelling you to show others His love. Your actions and engagement will be motivated by the love of God.

I prophesy to you today, that you flow with the love of God and it comes through your very being. May you show it with boldness and courage. I speak against unforgiveness, rage and violence. May you walk in love like never before and you will see the blessings of the Lord follow you greatly.

Galatians 5:13 - For, brethren, ye have been called unto liberty; only use not liberty for an occasion to the flesh, but by love serve one another.

SEPTEMBER 17

Today you will discover a revolution of alignment. You will become more open to the things that are in perfect alliance with your purpose. Relationships and behaviors are all coming into divine order for you. As they do you will begin to see and understand why all these things must be. The warfare will no longer be mysterious for you. You will know why you had to endure certain things in your life. Today God will make it all make sense.

I prophesy to you today, that you release yourself into this alignment for the future. You will no longer ask why but you will know what is of the mind and will of God concerning you. I speak to your mind that it be clearer than ever before. I speak to your will that you fully embrace this breakthrough.

Psalms 138:8 - The Lord will perfect that which concerneth me: thy mercy, O Lord, endureth for ever: forsake not the works of thine own hands.

SEPTEMBER 18

Today you will be promoted into another level of living. This elevation has been waiting for this day and now it's here. The Lord is prepared for you to live the life that He has ordained for you. All you had to do was survive to make it to today. Your endurance grants you access to the next level of living.

I prophesy to you today, that everything connected to your life receives elevation. Your money goes to the next level. Your health goes to the next level. Your desires are now in a new place and what used to satisfy you won't satisfy you anymore. Your taste buds have been adjusted by heaven and now God gives you what to desire. Today is the day your life receives an upgrade.

John 10:10 - The thief cometh not, but for to steal, and to kill, and to destroy: I am come that they might have life, and that they might have it more abundantly.

SEPTEMBER 19

Today is the day that your mind becomes more like the mind of God. You shall be thrust into a new way of thinking. This thinking is necessary for your future. The old thinking will not work on this level. Your decisions must line up with all that God is doing in your life right now. Your thinking is crucial. Be mindful of what you meditate or dwell on mentally. Things you think about too long will become a part of you. Be sure they reflect the things of God.

Today I prophesy to you, that you begin to make decisions that agree with your destiny. Your stable mind is key in this season. You will have to keep your mind stayed on the Lord. I command the peace of God and serenity of the Holy Spirit to rule your thoughts and your mind.

Ezekiel 11:5 - And the Spirit of the Lord fell upon me, and said unto me, Speak; Thus saith the Lord; Thus have ye said, O house of Israel: for I know the things that come into your mind, every one of them.

SEPTEMBER 20

Today is the day that you walk in to a new realm of completeness. You will burst forth into fulfillment like never before. You will begin to see doors and windows close in your life. Not as though you no longer have access, but because that door or window is complete and finished. You will no longer have too many unfinished projects in your life. God is giving you the grace to complete it.

I prophesy to you today, that you begin to breakthrough in to the realm called accomplishment. I speak to your tenacity and command it to increase. I speak to your levels of endurance and call forth strength to it. You will stick to the tasks until they are finished. Then you will begin to live life like never before, fulfilled and complete.

2 Timothy 3:17 - That the man of God may be perfect, thoroughly furnished unto all good works.

SEPTEMBER 21

Today you are being released into a new will. God has been working on you to convince you to change your will. Today your heart has been softened and you are being made newer. Your will is beginning to bow to the sovereignty of God. You are beginning to see things His way even the more. The lord has been compelling you and now your soul is answering the call.

I prophesy to you today, that you will surrender even more to what God has for you. I speak to you and request that you open your heart, mind and will to the new things that are right in front of you. You are the only one in complete control of your will. You must open it and allow it to be transform and changed by the power of the Holy Spirit. This is the only way you will see what is prepared for you. Be open today.

Revelation 3:20 - Behold, I stand at the door, and knock: if any man hear my voice, and open the door, I will come in to him, and will sup with him, and he with me.

SEPTEMBER 22

Today you are emancipated in to a happier life and living. The Lord has seen your secret sadness and He is coming for it, to change it and do away with it. It is the Lords desire to make you happy. He desires that as you please Him that you experience gladness and joy that flows throughout your entire life.

Today I prophesy to you, that you get a breakthrough in your spirit, so much so, that you have a new perception of life. It will cause you to smile more and be a lighter person to be around. People will desire to be around you because of your lighter spirit. I speak to the heaviness that has been weighing you down and command it to lift so that you may be free. It is so, in Jesus' Name!

John 13:17 - If ye know these things, happy are ye
if ye do them.

SEPTEMBER 23

Today you will break into production for what is to come. You will begin to receive a harvest on previously planted seeds. Those seeds will yield another harvest. The Lord will cause old seeds to produce again. Those seeds are producing again because there is something greater that is happening for you that you must walk into. What you will bring forth in this season will bring forth again and again. It will be a perpetual harvest for you.

I prophesy to you today, that you will be more productive in this season than in any other season. Get ready because a mighty harvest is about to break forth for you. I speak to old seeds you've sown over 20 years ago and I command them to germinate again and bring forth. I command it to produce more seeds for even more harvests.

Genesis 8:22 - While the earth remaineth, seedtime and harvest, and cold and heat, and summer and winter, and day and night shall not cease.

SEPTEMBER 24

Today is the day that you step strongly into your divine calling and purpose. You will begin to accept the call that is on your life and lean into it. You must welcome all that comes with it, for the Lord will be faithful to His promise concerning you. The Lord will prepare you and sharpen you for the assignment. You are being released into a priestly order for such a time as this.

Today, I prophesy to your spirit, to rise up within you to perform the good work to which you have been called. I send peace to you to protect you from all the woes you have perceived or even heard about ministry. May your yes outweigh you reluctance. You are called for now!

2 Timothy 1:9 - Who hath saved us, and called us with an holy calling, not according to our works, but according to his own purpose and grace, which was given us in Christ Jesus before the world began.

SEPTEMBER 25

Today you breakthrough into grace multiplied. Aforetime you were treated with harsh judgments and many inconsiderations. But the Lord has increased grace towards you and blessed you this day. His unmerited favor now follows you like a shadow in a bright sun light. You will not be able to escape the grace of our God. He has decided to do this thing to you and you will be abundantly blessed by His decisions.

Today I prophesy to your life, that it will be overtaken by the grace of God. I speak to everything that pertains to you. I command it all to be effected by the grace of God. Your family and your possessions will all be kissed by the favor that God decides to release in your life this day.

Romans 6:14 - For sin shall not have dominion over you: for ye are not under the law, but under grace.

SEPTEMBER 26

Today you will break forth into your god-likeness. People around you will begin to see the god-nature in you. You will show forth the goodness and mercy of God so much that your light will begin to shine brighter. Prepare to be transformed more and more. God will rise up within you until your image is as the image of Christ. That is His goal and He will work until it is done.

I prophesy to you today, that you begin to lay aside everything that doesn't look like God. May you boldly put aside all behaviors and actions that are contrary to your divine nature. Zion is calling you to a higher place of praise. You must answer this call in your very identity until your DNA reflects what God designed it to be before you came forth out of your mother's womb.

2 Corinthians 4:4 - In whom the god of this world hath blinded the minds of them which believe not, lest the light of the glorious gospel of Christ, who is the image of God, should shine unto them.

SEPTEMBER 27

Today you will breakthrough into a deeper relationship with God. The Lord desires to have a closer walk with you and you have desired more of Him. Today is the day that your prayer will be answered. God will begin to reveal to you the many benefits of walking closer to Him. You will embrace a new love for God that you have never possessed before. Today the power of your relationship with God will open doors to new realms of peace and joy.

I prophesy to you today, that you will experience the joy of your salvation and that joy will release you into a greater desire for the Lord. May you release yourself into the fullness of what the Lord has for you. I speak to your spirit that it has an insatiable desire for the Lord that develops new levels of faithfulness in your walk with Him.

Deuteronomy 5:33 - Ye shall walk in all the ways which the Lord your God hath commanded you, that ye may live, and that it may be well with you, and that ye may prolong your days in the land which ye shall possess.

SEPTEMBER 28

Today is the day that you breakthrough in to mastering your skills. The Lord has been developing you in the areas of your expertise. Every situation and encounter you've had has been preparing you for this season. This mastery will release you in to areas of influence and you will be in much demand. This will give you opportunity to show forth the goodness of the Lord and for the Lord to glorify Himself through your gifts.

Today I prophesy to you, that you throw yourself into greater levels of preparation and development. As you rehearse your gifts, you will see how the Lord will use them to His glory. Make intentional investments into your skills as it will give you a great return and the Lords name will be made great through you in the earth.

Deuteronomy 18:13 - Thou shalt be perfect with the Lord thy God.

SEPTEMBER 29

Today is the day to release yourself into transformation. You have been avoiding change as it has frightened you as to what it would look like. But today, your faith rises to make the necessary changes to obtain the transformation that will reveal what you have been destined for. God is doing a greater work within you and making life adjustments will launch the greatness.

I prophesy to you today, that you be not afraid of change any longer. You are breaking through the staleness and stagnation that has held you back. You are being released out of the prison of the mundane and the old. There is a freshness being revealed in the changes you are about to make. This is the will of God for you.

Hebrews 7:12 - For the priesthood being changed, there is made of necessity a change also of the law.

SEPTEMBER 30

Today is the day that you discovery new levels of consecration. The Lord is calling you to a higher place of dedication so that He may use you. You are being separated for purpose and for a holy use. Today you must make a decision to separate yourself unto the Lord for His Glory.

I prophesy to you today, that you begin to develop a lifestyle of holiness and sanctification. You are in this world but you are not of this world. There is a divine mandate that has been given to you of the Lord. He wants you unto Himself. As you answer His call you will be satisfied in the deepest parts of your being.

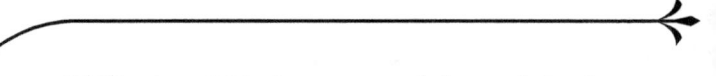

Philippians 3:14 - I press toward the mark for the prize of the high calling of God in Christ Jesus.

OCTOBER

"The Month of Natural Order"

OCTOBER 1

Today is the day that your natural life aligns with God. There will be a divine influence within your day that causes you to affiliate with what God has determined for your life. Everything you consider to be insignificant or minuscule will be subjective by the Holy Spirit. God will cause your life to be swayed by His presence and you will see drastic changes of development.

I prophesy today, that you begin to submit all of your affairs to God. Do not only give Him the greater matters, but also surrender to Him the smaller ones. Allow the Lord God to impact your every decision. Permit the Holy Spirit to choose on your behalf even the situations you believe to be common. As you do so, you will begin to walk in a new order of God that will release supernatural favor.

1 Corinthians 2:14 - But the natural man receiveth not the things of the Spirit of God: for they are foolishness unto him: neither can he know them, because they are spiritually discerned.

OCTOBER 2

Today you will begin to witness your life in a new flow. You will experience people blessing you and giving you favor. This entire month you will see people sent to you to be a blessing in your life. They will use their influence to give you favor and success. The Lord has ordered this for you.

I prophesy today, that you begin to receive what the Lord has ordered for you from the hands of men. There are people that have been marked by heaven to move on your behalf. God has sanctioned this to be so and it begins today. Open your heart and your hand to receive these rewards and blessings.

Luke 6:38 - Give, and it shall be given unto you; good measure, pressed down, and shaken together, and running over, shall men give into your bosom. For with the same measure that ye mete withal it shall be measured to you again.

OCTOBER 3

Today is the day that you move into agreement with all of heaven. Your life will reflect what is occurring in heaven. The changes that are being made to your personage is becoming a reflection of the design of God for you. There is a holy transformation that is occurring.

Today, I prophesy, that as you witness the trees changing color and the weather changing, so shall these changes be within you. God is causing you to experience newness and it is a result of what heaven has determined for you. I speak over your mind, your body and your spirit that they all welcome the changes that are taking place. God is changing your tone and your hues so that you may show His glory in the earth.

Matthew 6:10 - Thy kingdom come. Thy will be done in earth, as it is in heaven.

OCTOBER 4

Today is the day to be stretched. You will begin to experience challenges that will seemingly come from nowhere. But these are stretching opportunities. God desires to show you what He has placed within you. The only way you will notice it- is when you're faced with challenges you believe to be beyond your capacity. But you will see what you can do.

I prophesy, that today you allow your mind to stretch beyond how you used to think. I speak to your spirit that it begins to explore God in new ways and your faith be stretched to new dimensions. I announce to your heart that you will not exist in fear but faith is your fuel for your life. Be stretched for the greater work and the greater life.

Matthew 12:13 - Then saith he to the man, Stretch forth thine hand. And he stretched it forth; and it was restored whole, like as the other.

OCTOBER 5

Today is the day that God graces your decisions. You have been toiling with making a decision for the next season of your life. You have been warring with what to do and how to do it. The Lord says to you today to make a decision and He will grace it. You will have the grace to complete the task with success.

I prophesy today, that you begin to have clear thoughts and presence of mind to decide what you should do. I rebuke fear and anxiety that causes you to be afraid of your own decisions. I speak deliverance into you, to be free from the erred choices of your past. You will decide correctly this time and it will work for your good. You have Gods grace!

John 15:16 - You did not choose me, but I chose you and appointed you that you should go and bear fruit and that your fruit should abide, so that whatever you ask the Father in my name, he may give it to you.

OCTOBER 6

Today God moves upon the hearts of those who are in power to make decisions for your favor. Though they may not be aware, God has led them to make laws and rules that will most benefit you. God has given them directions to turn legislation in your favor. Politicians, supervisors, employers and rulers alike will begin to extend to you grace and favor that is uncommon. Your life will be completely affected by these new decrees.

Today I prophesy to you, begin to position your self for increase. Begin to open your arms and hands to receive what the Lord has declared in your life. Your eyes will see change and your pockets will receive overflow. The mouth of the Lord has declared it.

Proverbs 21:1 - The king's heart is in the hand of the Lord, as the rivers of water: he turneth it whithersoever he will.

OCTOBER 7

Today is the day that your healing becomes complete. You have been in recovery from past wounds and hurts. The things that have tortured and tormented you for a while are coming to a close. Old sores won't hurt any longer. Old wounds are closing and healing up today. You will see that former triggers are present no longer. Your healing is becoming complete and you're being released from the recovery room.

I prophesy, that you will begin to exercise the muscles that you haven't moved in some time now. I speak to your process and your pain. As you move into the things of God you will see that the things that used to hurt, doesn't any longer. You were in recovery, but now you are in victory!

Isaiah 38:9 - The writing of Hezekiah king of Judah, when he had been sick, and was recovered of his sickness:

OCTOBER 8

Today is the day that you will experience a renewal in your life. You are stepping into a new order of things concerning you. You are beginning to reassess your life and what you have produced. It provokes a divine reset, which will become like a new beginning for you. Get ready to embrace a new order of things.

I prophesy that today you begin to walk in a new perspective, new perception and new insight concerning your life. I speak to your eyes that they see sharply into your future to create a motivation for your movements today. Grab hold of what is to come, for it begins today!

Haggai 1:7 - Thus saith the Lord of hosts;
Consider your ways.

OCTOBER 9

Today is the day to embrace a new order of breakthrough. The lord will begin to cause you to obtain the future you desire, but using unconventional ways and means. The way you used to get results will be no more. The Lord is opening new avenues and ways to get better results, but its going to require that you be adaptable and flexible to the different route He will use.

Today, I prophesy that you begin to open your eyes to see the new people and new methods that the Lord will use to bless you. It is new to you, but it is not new to God. He is opening up unusual doors for you and this is the season to walk therein.

Ezekiel 46:3 - Likewise the people of the land shall worship at the door of this gate before the Lord in the sabbaths and in the new moons.

OCTOBER 10

Today the Lord begins to partner you with people who are prepared for change and who share like passions as you do. Your journey to find your tribe is being manifested today. You will begin to embrace relationships with those who are going after similar things and whose goals align with yours. Today is the day for new relationships.

I prophesy to you today, that you wear the fragrance that is attractive to successful people and to those who are designed to assist you in your next. I speak that you carry the presence of someone who is prepared for the future and simply needs to connect with those who are ready to make positive changes.

Acts 14:15 - And saying, Sirs, why do ye these things? We also are men of like passions with you, and preach unto you that ye should turn from these vanities unto the living God, which made heaven, and earth, and the sea, and all things that are therein:

OCTOBER 11

Today is the day that the lord deals with your inadequacies and the areas of your life that you perceive you're inadequate in. The enemy has been working overtime to throw in your face and remind you of the areas that you don't perform well in. But God has waged war on this effort today and heaven begins to send an onslaught of encouragement your way. Your confidence is beginning to grow and increase today and more and more each day.

I prophesy today, that you begin to cast away all thoughts and ideas of incompetency. Today I rebuke insecurity, the lack of confidence and misperception from off of you. May you being to see yourself in the light of revelation from God. Today you tap into the revelation that you are enough and are qualified for what God has coming your way.

Judges 6:16 - And the Lord said unto him, Surely I will be with thee, and thou shalt smite the Midianites as one man.

OCTOBER 12

Be prepared to witness the convergence of heaven and earth. Today is the day that the Lord impacts your life and causes you to be completely influenced by His will. All that God has for you is unfolding and colliding with your decisions and intentions. You will be overcome by the need to please the lord. In return, God has on His agenda only to satisfy the longing of your soul.

I speak over you today the willingness to allow God to take over your entire being. I prophesy to you today, that there be a great sense of peace concerning what the lord is doing within you in this season. May you accept the burden of blessings that is about to flow your way.

Deuteronomy 28:2 - And all these blessings shall come on thee, and overtake thee, if thou shalt hearken unto the voice of the Lord thy God.

OCTOBER 13

Today, may you become more aware of the things that come naturally to you. Your future is hidden in your daily routine. The lord has been trying to show you your purpose, but you have been blinded by normality. It's what comes normal to you, the thing that you are called to. Your purpose is within who you organically are. Today is the day to discover it and pay close attention to it.

I prophesy to you today, that you do not fight against the thing that you are called to do. I speak over your will to surrender to the purpose of God on your life. May your natural gifts no longer get resistance from you. May they all come forth and manifest in the earth to glorify God.

Isaiah 41:9 - Thou whom I have taken from the ends of the earth, and called thee from the chief men thereof, and said unto thee, Thou art my servant; I have chosen thee, and not cast thee away.

OCTOBER 14

Today will be the day that you will come in contact with people who can and will bless you. Whoever isn't for you wont find you and who is for you wont miss you. On this day you will discover new connections and moments will matter in meeting new people. The Lord is sending divine connections your way.

I prophesy today, that you do not let these relationships pass you by. I speak to your heart that you be healed from the traumas of the past encounters so that you may allow new ones to connect to you. May you be in perfect timing and in the perfect location for the connection to occur. Today your steps are ordered and the blessing will not pass over you.

2 Kings 10:15 - And when he was departed thence, he lighted on Jehonadab the son of Rechab coming to meet him: and he saluted him, and said to him, Is thine heart right, as my heart is with thy heart? And Jehonadab answered, It is. If it be, give me thine hand. And he gave him his hand; and he took him up to him into the chariot.

OCTOBER 15

On this day you must take control of your time of rest! You must make it your business to include a time of Sabbath in your schedule. Your rest is imperative to your success. Your rest contributes to your RESToration. If you don't rest, you wont be creative and innovative. God is compelling you to make the time to settle your body and your mind so that He may minister to it and you can be rejuvenated.

I prophesy that you are courageous enough to make the time to rest today. All of your competing commitments will be there once you are restored. You will handle them with sharpness and precision once your body has been refueled. You have a mandate to rest and it is your responsibility to do it.

Job 11:18 - And thou shalt be secure, because there is hope; yea, thou shalt dig about thee, and thou shalt take thy rest in safety.

OCTOBER 16

Today is the day to reach out to those that you love. Allow them to hear your heart and sense your love for them. Don't be afraid to say 'I love you' to those who you love. The Lord has expressed His love to you and His desire is that you distribute His love to others. Show the love of God on purpose. Even to those that you don't know. Express God's love to others in a tangible way.

I prophesy today, that you begin to be bold enough to love and love again. I speak to your heart that it is overwhelmed with the love of God and that you have no other choice but to share it with others. May you be courageous enough to even love difficult people or those who have wronged you. This will be evidence of your healing and lead you in the right path of breakthrough.

John 13:34 - A new commandment I give unto you, That ye love one another; as I have loved you, that ye also love one another.

OCTOBER 17

Today is the day that your journey aligns with your destiny. It will not be déjà vu. It will be the natural order of things aligning with the divine order of things. Your entire life has not been by circumstance or mistake. It has been the lord who has controlled your steps and your experiences. It will all begin to make sense today why you had to encounter the things you did.

I prophesy that today is a good day for you. You will feel good in your body and your soul. You will feel productive and accomplished. Without doing particular tasks there is a sense of fulfillment that will come over you. It is God bringing the order of things into perfect agreement with each other. He has ordained this to be.

Ephesians 2:10 - For we are his workmanship, created in Christ Jesus unto good works, which God hath before ordained that we should walk in them.

OCTOBER 18

Today is a day to pay attention to your health. Healing is the lord's responsibility but good health is your responsibility. As the holidays are approaching, you must begin to make sure your body is healthy to carry out your assignments. Eating unhealthy will rob you of this opportunity. Don't think of dieting, but think of life adjustments that are necessary for you to have a future. Do not eat according to your desires but eat according to your destiny.

Today I prophesy that you are able to develop a discipline to eat, exercise and meditate on the word of God intentionally. May your plate look like your purpose. May you begin to have a change of palate and your desires begin to align with your calling. I break the covenants with food addiction off your life. May slothfulness and laziness no longer be your ally. You are limber, agile, healthy, whole and you have a sound mind.

1 Corinthians 10:31 - Whether therefore ye eat, or drink, or whatsoever ye do, do all to the glory of God.

OCTOBER 19

Today God makes a decision for you. You have been between two opinions on certain matters and haven't been able to make up your mind. But the Lord makes the choice for you. It is best for your purpose and your future. The Lord knows what lies ahead and He will decide according to that. All you have to do is agree with what He decides.

Today I prophesy to you, allow the decisions of God to prevail in your life. Don't fight what is happening, for it is the choice blessings of God. Though it may not look that way at first, you will see how it will all work together for your good. The Lord is omniscient concerning you. He knows the end before the beginning. Trust Him and trust in Him. He will not fail you.

Proverbs 16:9 - A man's heart deviseth his way:
but the Lord directeth his steps.

OCTOBER 20

Today is the day of remuneration for you. What has been owed to you will come to you. The lord has defended you and you have found favor in His sight. He has caused the enemy to repay you for all the trials and damage he has caused. Your home, your family and your possessions will receive payment. The hand of the enemy has been rebuked and the devour has been devoured. Today vindication comes to your house.

I prophesy to you today to sit back and receive. You will receive the just reward of your patience and God's concern of you. The Lord has seen the injustice served to you and has reversed the sentence. And now you will be blessed because of the last season of the enemy's trespasses. God will make him repay you. Just receive. Do not gloat or brag. But rather make your boast in the lord. It is He that has made this happen for you.

Hebrews 2:2 - For if the word spoken by angels was stedfast, and every transgression and disobedience received a just recompence of reward;

OCTOBER 21

Today may your discernment be sharpened that you will see the wickedness of others towards you. There are some who have chosen to be used of the enemy to come against you. The Lord will fight for you and the spirit that is motivating them will be broken. You must behave yourself wisely and in a perfect way. Do not allow their ways to compel you to react the same. Your maturity in the things of God will be crucial to your victory.

I prophesy today, that you not allow the willful wickedness of others to contaminate your heart and spirit. Be bold enough to return evil for good and to study to be quiet. This is a spiritual battle and you will prevail if you follow the leading of the Lord and not your emotions.

Ephesians 6:12 - For we wrestle not against flesh and blood, but against principalities, against powers, against the rulers of the darkness of this world, against spiritual wickedness in high places.

OCTOBER 22

Today the spirit of philanthropy comes upon you. A givers heart is within you. The lord has blessed you to be a blessing. You are designed to distribute the blessing to others. The lord causes great things to come your way so that you may share the favor with others. Be led of the lord as to who to bless and who to communicate the blessing with. He will lead you. He desires to get the blessing to others through you. You are a blessing agent.

I prophesy to you today to open your heart and your hand. The lord wants to use you as a conduit of favor. I speak to your barns that they are filled with plenty. I speak to your storehouse that it is overflowing. I speak to your wealth that it increases more and more. The blessing is more than you have room to receive. Now prepare to bless others.

Genesis 12:2 - And I will make of thee a great nation, and I will bless thee, and make thy name great; and thou shalt be a blessing:

OCTOBER 23

It is harvest season for you! You have entered into a time where the fruit of your labor will be manifested. You will see the results of your hard work and toiling. The lord has caused you to bear fruit and to now bring it forth. Your field will not be barren nor will your labor be desolate. Harvest time has come for you. Your seed will produce more seed. Your harvest will be perpetual. For many seasons you will experience plenty.

I prophesy to you today, that you become a harvest manager. You will know what to do in this season. You will know what to store up and what to consume. You will know what to give away and what to keep. There is a holy wisdom that comes upon you to make you liken unto Joseph. Your families will be blessed by this wisdom that you possess.

John 15:8 - Herein is my Father glorified, that ye bear much fruit; so shall ye be my disciples.

OCTOBER 24

Today is the day to walk in your divine calling. Today you must embrace the things that God has ordained for you to do. There is a priestly order that you are called to. There is service to humanity that you have been chosen for. You must discover it, embrace it and exercise it. You can no longer resist this holy mandate. Accepting it will release new levels of peace into your life.

I prophesy that today you begin to move in the direction of yielding. May you surrender to the will of God completely. There are people that are awaiting your 'yes' to God. Their lives will be blessed by it. There are communities that will change as a result of your willingness to comply with holy orders. Don't hold them up any longer.

2 Timothy 1:9 - Who hath saved us, and called us with an holy calling, not according to our works, but according to his own purpose and grace, which was given us in Christ Jesus before the world began,

OCTOBER 25

Today is the day to extend grace. You must first extend grace to yourself. Give yourself the same thing the Lord gives you. The lord is gracious to you. Be gracious to yourself. Do not be quick to cast judgment or develop a harsh perception of yourself, but show yourself grace. Then extend that grace to others. Show others the grace that you have seen the lord show towards you. If you are the recipient of grace then you need to show grace.

I prophesy to you today, that you rid your heart and mind from the inclination to be unforgiving or harsh. May you begin to be overwhelmed with a sense of kindness and favor. May grace become your life's fragrance. Allow grace to go with you everywhere you go. You will then behold a new heart that pleases the lord.

Romans 5:15 - But not as the offence, so also is the free gift. For if through the offence of one many be dead, much more the grace of God, and the gift by grace, which is by one man, Jesus Christ, hath abounded unto many.

OCTOBER 26

Today is the day that you begin to transform into the image of God even the more. All of the insecurities that you've had about yourself will begin to experience a transformation. You will start to feel things change for you in the realms of your self-perception. The image of God will become more and more attractive to you. It will rise from within you and will manifest even on the outside.

I prophesy to you today that you allow yourself to go through this metamorphosis. Allow yourself to go through this beautiful change into the image that God has set in Jesus Christ. Begin to embrace the new you. It will assist you in building your confidence and esteem.

Hebrews 10:35 - Cast not away therefore your confidence, which hath great recompence of reward.

OCTOBER 27

Today is the day you experience the power of Gods salvation in your whole being. Everything that concerns you will be touched by God's power. You will experience change, breakthrough, healing, deliverance, love, grace and favor. All of your being is affected by the fullness of God. There are areas of your life that will never be the same again. Your faith increases to allow the fullness of God to come forth and touch you and minister to you.

I prophesy to you today, that the power of Calvary walks with you and overtakes you. I speak to your very being that you sense the power of the saving cross of Jesus. May you begin to be engulfed with His love for you and receive the innumerable benefits of His death, burial and resurrection. May each part of you be blessed beyond measure.

Romans 5:10 - For if, when we were enemies, we were reconciled to God by the death of his Son, much more, being reconciled, we shall be saved by his life.

OCTOBER 28

Today you are being released from perfectionism. You have bound yourself into the barracks of failure or incompleteness due to your need to be perfect. You haven't given yourself enough grace or enough credit. But today you are being made free from that perception. God is working on your level of grace towards yourself and He desires that you show yourself the grace He affords you. No longer will you have to have everything perfect in order to progress and move forward.

I prophesy today, that you have a change of heart and a change of mind concerning the need to be perfect at all times. I speak to your mind that you receive transformation and peace. I speak to your emotions that you be made free from the harsh judgments you've made concerning yourself. Your anxiety levels are being made low and your esteem is rising this day. God is granting you His peace and it comforts your very soul.

John 14:27 - Peace I leave with you, my peace I give unto you: not as the world giveth, give I unto you. Let not your heart be troubled, neither let it be afraid.

OCTOBER 29

As you witness the change in the seasons, so will you see the change within you even the more. Today is the day that change is manifested within you. This season will seem very uncertain because you are experiencing so many changes. Do not make any long term decisions right now. Things in your life are still varying. Once they settle out, you will be able to make better decisions for the future. These changes will only benefit you and bless you. God is behind it all. He has ordered this for you.

Today I prophesy to you that you allow yourself to be adjusted in the ways that benefit you most. I speak over your will, that it complies with the will of God. I speak to your trust levels that you begin to trust God more and more. Change is good and this is your good season.

Zechariah 3:4 - And he answered and spake unto those that stood before him, saying, Take away the filthy garments from him. And unto him he said, Behold, I have caused thine iniquity to pass from thee, and I will clothe thee with change of raiment.

OCTOBER 30

Today is the day you become more involved with wisdom. Your age and your experiences have all contributed to your wisdom level. God gives it to you freely and you will freely engage it. Wisdom will have her perfect work in you. Your decisions and your thinking will all be fully enveloped in wisdom. You will be sought after to offer wise counsel to many. They will bless you for the wisdom you possess.

I prophesy to you today that you carry the grace of the sage. May you open your mind to see things as they are and know what to do. May you be able to properly apply the knowledge you have. I speak to your discernment of timing that you are able to move within the timing of God.

Proverbs 4:7 - Wisdom is the principal thing; therefore get wisdom: and with all thy getting get understanding.

OCTOBER 31

Today is the day that you become familiar with the name of God. He will reveal Himself to you in new ways. Therefore, you will know Him as you have never before. As you know His name, be sure to exalt His name. Your goal will be to know Him and to make Him known. You will spread His name throughout the earth and many will come to know Him because of your testimony of Him.

I prophesy to you today, that you become more acquainted with God. May your prayer life increase. May your time of prayer increase. May your devotion and communion with Him go higher. This will result in your knowledge of who He is and in return you will share with everyone you know the greatness of our God.

Luke 1:49 - For he that is mighty hath done to me great things; and holy is his name.

NOVEMBER

"The Month of Persistence"

NOVEMBER 1

Today is the day that you must pursue God with tenacity. There are many things that He desires to show you and do within you. Your answers lie within Him. As you follow hard after Him, you will begin to receive all that He has planned and prepared for you. Your pursuit of God will not be distracted nor will it be diverted. Your eyes and heart will not be satisfied until it has reached the goal of God.

I prophesy that today you develop a hunger and a thirst for God like never before. I speak to your heart that it develops a longing for God that can only be quenched by God. May you want Him more and more until your only desire in life is Him. You will not only want from Him, but you will grow to a place that you want only Him.

Psalms 42:1 - As the hart panteth after the water brooks, so panteth my soul after thee, O God.

NOVEMBER 2

Today is the day that you commit to tell your story. You will share your story of God's amazing grace and power. You will share of His great work in your life. You will no longer see yourself as a victim, but victorious through Jesus Christ. This will not be a story of victimization, but a testimony of triumph. As you share it with others, the fear of the Lord will increase throughout the region.

I prophesy to you today, that your life be rid of shame and embarrassment of your story. I speak a holy boldness to take over you that you are willing to share it with everyone you meet. May your mouth be worded with the potency of Gods love and work in your life. May you become divinely compelled to speak of the wonderful works of God to family, friends, strangers and everyone you meet.

John 4:29 - Come, see a man, which told me all things that ever I did: is not this the Christ?

NOVEMBER 3

Today is the day that your diligence for the fullness of God pays off. God in all of His glory is making Himself available to you and He is at your disposal. The Father, The Son and the Holy Spirit is before you and is meeting you at your point of desire of Him. Be pursuant to all of Him so that you may be graced with all that He is doing in your life in this season.

I prophesy, that you begin to explore the deep things of God. I speak to your heart that you open up and let all of God in. I speak to your spirit that you welcome in the Spirit of God to fellowship and commune with you.

Ephesians 3:19 - And to know the love of Christ, which passeth knowledge, that ye might be filled with all the fulness of God.

NOVEMBER 4

Today the winds are determined to blow in your direction. They will not miss you nor will they blow over you. They will flow in your life to bring about the favor of God. The winds of heaven are blowing today on your behalf. God has spoken to the winds and have commanded them to send blessings your way. He has determined to send the winds of the heavens on assignment for you.

I prophesy to you today that you become stabilized in this season, that you are able to stand when the winds of God blows. I speak strong footing and sure steps so that the winds will bless you and not burden you. God will do what He said concerning you and you will see it with your own eyes.

Ezekiel 37:9 - Then said he unto me, Prophesy unto the wind, prophesy, son of man, and say to the wind, Thus saith the Lord God; Come from the four winds, O breath, and breathe upon these slain, that they may live.

NOVEMBER 5

Today is the day for stubborn favor to come your way. God has made favor stubborn for you. It will not stop until it has accomplished full favor in your life. Favor has been ordered of the lord to pursue you and overtake you. This is the day you will see it unfold and manifest. Favor has been commanded to come to your address, your body and your business. You are the target of favor. It will not miss! No one else can get this favor that has been determined for you. It won't go anywhere else. Your name is on it.

I prophesy to you today that you stand in the assurance that you are favors target. You have been marked for the favor of God. I pray that you welcome all of its benefits and that you receive all that it has to offer. Be prepared to be full and experience the overflow of this uncommon favor.

Acts 7:46 - Who found favour before God, and desired to find a tabernacle for the God of Jacob.

NOVEMBER 6

Today is the day to increase your persistency. You must become more determined to achieve your goals and the things of God. As you do this you will discover new levels of fulfillment. Your determination will be met with great rewards. Being persistent will pay off in this season. You cannot give up, but you must continue.

I prophesy today that you receive the strength to continue in spite of what's going on around you. May your will outweigh your war. I speak to your ability to withstand adversity. May it increase significantly and your tolerance for pain become higher. You will surprise yourself as to what you can withstand in this season. It is all due to your strong desire to get to your intended goals.

Isaiah 50:7 - For the Lord God will help me;
therefore shall I not be confounded: therefore
have I set my face like a flint, and I know that I
shall not be ashamed.

NOVEMBER 7

Not only will you be persistent, but also there is a resolve within you to complete and finish. No longer will things go unmet or unfinished in your life. You are birthing an innate desire to complete tasks, assignments, reach goals and finish projects. You will no longer start but not finish. God has graced you with the ability to see things through until the end. Today your name changes to 'The Finisher'. You will be complete, therefore you will complete.

I prophesy to you today, that you organize your priorities and align your purpose with your routines. You are a life manager and you are able to manage things well. This will all contribute to your ability to complete and finish tasks. May your heart only be settled when things are done. Until then, may you have the strength and bandwidth to finish.

Philippians 1:6 - Being confident of this very thing, that he which hath begun a good work in you will perform it until the day of Jesus Christ:

NOVEMBER 8

Today is the day to go back to the drawing board concerning some of your plans. In this season you need to revisit some ideas and begin again. Don't give up nor put it off. You simply need to start all over. This is a good time for you to rethink your approach, as the lord will grace you with the ability to start again. You have not failed, you have not done anything wrong, you simply need to start all over because of the change of times and seasons.

I prophesy to you today that you take courage and be encouraged. I speak over your mind and heart that you are bold enough to plan again and pick up old visions. I speak the mind of Christ within you to humbly think of yourself as servant and reassess your role in the future. There you will discover your purpose. You have been graced to start all over and it begins today.

Acts 3:19 - Repent ye therefore, and be converted, that your sins may be blotted out, when the times of refreshing shall come from the presence of the Lord;

NOVEMBER 9

Today is the day to fight for your breakthrough. There has been much warfare concerning your deliverance. There has been a stronghold on you to keep you stagnant. But you must be more determined than the bondage. Your desire for your freedom must outweigh the oppression. Once the enemy has seen that you are determined and will not let up, they will relinquish their hold. You must continue to fight.

I prophesy today, that you put on the whole armor of God and be strong in the Lord and in the power of His might. The lord will fight with you and even fight for you, but you must be determined. This is the day to fight through feelings and emotions. You will get the victory and this will be over soon. God will give you the freedom you desire.

Hebrews 11:34 - Quenched the violence of fire, escaped the edge of the sword, out of weakness were made strong, waxed valiant in fight, turned to flight the armies of the aliens.

NOVEMBER 10

Today God will deal with the stubborn laws and judgments against you. Those things that have been hard to move and would not allow you to experience peace and freedom, He will remove out of your way. The Lord begins to remove the strongman and the hindrances from around you. He will cause the high places to be made low. You have been under the strong hand of the wicked, but you are being released today.

I prophesy to you today that you be released from under the rule of wicked people and institutions. Today I speak over your entire being that you experience freedom from oppressive forces and powers. Be made free and enjoy the joy and peace of the lord.

Isaiah 42:16 - And I will bring the blind by a way that they knew not; I will lead them in paths that they have not known: I will make darkness light before them, and crooked things straight. These things will I do unto them, and not forsake them.

NOVEMBER 11

Today is the day that you receive the strength to be unwavering. You will not let up concerning your goals, visions and dreams. You must be relentless in this hour. You will see it all come to pass, but it will take all that you are to see it. God will strengthen you to keep at it and never to give up.

Today, I prophesy that you be persistent and unmoving. Your focus will be key for you. As you focus, you will see the things you desire be made manifest. You will see it and your will to concentrate will cause it to come. Your enemy will be distractions. As long as you choose not to be distracted, you will obtain the victory.

1 Corinthians 15:58 - Therefore, my beloved brethren, be ye stedfast, unmoveable, always abounding in the work of the Lord, forasmuch as ye know that your labour is not in vain in the Lord.

NOVEMBER 12

Today is the day that God moves on your behalf and He will not let up on you. He will block every wrong path and make clear the right path for you to go in. This is the season that God will make it impossible for you to make the wrong decisions and moves. You will see the determination of God for you. His desire for your deliverance is far greater than even your own.

Today I prophesy, that you allow God to do His will and bidding in your life. You will see how firm God is towards you. May you walk in the blessings and the favor He has waiting for you on the other side of this. May you begin to see it all unfold and accept it as the blessing of the lord.

Ezekiel 24:14 - I the Lord have spoken it: it shall come to pass, and I will do it; I will not go back, neither will I spare, neither will I repent; according to thy ways, and according to thy doings, shall they judge thee, saith the Lord God.

NOVEMBER 13

Today is the day to rebel against procrastination. You must fight against putting things off to later. There must be a determination within you to get things done. You must fight any urge to delay tasks. Place projects in order of priority and get the high priority responsibilities done. God will guide you with His hand in the way he wants you to go. You will not fail in this season. But you must not move slowly. You must make haste and be intentional. It will yield great rewards.

I prophesy to you today, that you have fortitude to be focused and a will to be active. Even being proactive will compensate you in large ways. I speak to your mind to be sharp and your thoughts to be clear. This will be a season to get things done and the next season will be nothing but the fruit of this one.

1 Samuel 20:38 - And Jonathan cried after the lad, Make speed, haste, stay not. And Jonathan's lad gathered up the arrows, and came to his master.

NOVEMBER 14

Today is the day that you receive the willpower to forgive. There have been things that you have held on to that you need to let go. You have owned your pain and owned the moment of the offense. But it has held you back from so many opportunities. But today is the day you become bold enough to release it and the person who caused it.

I prophesy to you today that you begin to untie yourself from the moment of your trauma and pain. The Lord sends help your way to deliver you. I speak over your heart that you be healed and I command you to courageously release the hurt. May your mouth utter the words of forgiveness that your heart has now achieved.

2 Corinthians 2:10 - To whom ye forgive any thing, I forgive also: for if I forgave any thing, to whom I forgave it, for your sakes forgave I it in the person of Christ;

NOVEMBER 15

Now is the time that you fight to get rest. Today begins the first day that you schedule rest and a time of Sabbath. Your future is being threatened by a lack of rest. Your mind will be sharper and your body will be restored when you do. Things have come to distract you or hinder your time of rest. But you must be practical and schedule it and be intentional about keeping the schedule.

I prophesy today, that you become restored and rejuvenated through the gift of rest. May rest be your portion and a refreshing be your meat. May your mind be clearer as a result. I speak over your day and I command it to loose the clock and expose the time leeches that hinder a time of rest. The Lord God will bless you and time will be your ally.

Mark 6:31 - And he said unto them, Come ye yourselves apart into a desert place, and rest a while: for there were many coming and going, and they had no leisure so much as to eat.

NOVEMBER 16

Today is the day to love on those who are particularly difficult. It is easy to express love to those who are lovable, but today the Lord desires that you show His love to those who are not as lovable. Even within your family dynamic, there are those who it has been challenging to reach or get to. Be intentional about loving them today as God will use you to draw them closer to Him.

I prophesy to you today, that you become relentless in loving others. No matter what they have done or the condition they are in, your goal is to love them and show them love. As you commit to this regardless of circumstances, you will see souls come to know the lord in a pure way. Your eyes will see how God can use you to bring others to Him.

Romans 5:8 - But God commendeth his love
toward us, in that, while we were yet sinners,
Christ died for us.

NOVEMBER 17

Today is the day to break stubborn alignments. You have affiliated yourself with things and people that are not flexible to the change you are experiencing. It has become a burden to you to adjust but remain connected to things that won't adapt. But today you will cease these covenants and walk into a liberty of growth and expansion. God has sent His word before you and has commanded the angels to assist.

I prophesy to you today, that you begin to recognize your future and that you disassociate yourself from the things that are not in agreement with where you are going. I speak over your will and your personality. May your addiction to the past or the familiar be broken and you be made free today.

1 Corinthians 15:33 - Be not deceived: evil communications corrupt good manners.

NOVEMBER 18

Today is the day to remove everything from your life that is robbing you of life. You must pay attention to the things that cause you agony, anxiety and anger and eliminate them expeditiously. God is the giver of life and He has given you an abundant life. Today is the day to take it fully and completely.

I prophesy that today you begin to live. I speak life to you and within you. The abundant life. The good life and a free life. May you take away everything that is zapping your life from you and do away with them. I speak to your boldness and command it to rise up to make this courageous move.

2 Peter 1:3 - According as his divine power hath given unto us all things that pertain unto life and godliness, through the knowledge of him that hath called us to glory and virtue:

NOVEMBER 19

Today is the day to walk in all that God has decided for you. Do not war or fight against it. The Lord has decided a thing for you and you must not become an enemy against it. Today, choose to be convinced that the will of God is better, bigger and greater for you. He knows and understands all things. When you trust in His decisions and choices for your life you will walk in the blessings that come with it.

I prophesy to you today, to trust completely in the selections of God. I speak to your ability to rely upon Him for all things, that it is like never before. I command your heart to trust and hope in Him for all of your cares. As you do this, you will see the benefits and blessings to follow.

2 Samuel 22:31 - As for God, his way is perfect; the word of the Lord is tried: he is a buckler to all them that trust in him.

NOVEMBER 20

Today you will walk in full redemption. Everything that was lost will be redeemed. Everything that was stolen will be restored. The wait is over for you to do without the things that God has determined for you. They will come to you like rain and overshadow you. You will no longer do without them. They will come to you again and you will possess them.

I prophesy to you today, that you receive total recall on your possessions. I speak to the winds of the earth and command them to loose your stuff. I command every enemy that has stolen from you to relinquish your possessions and deliver them back to your hands. I speak to the lost things and I command them to be found again. Your time of redemption has come.

Exodus 6:6 - Wherefore say unto the children of Israel, I am the Lord, and I will bring you out from under the burdens of the Egyptians, and I will rid you out of their bondage, and I will redeem you with a stretched out arm, and with great judgments:

NOVEMBER 21

Today a willful wickedness will come to an end. The lord will rise up within you and overtake the nature that is willing to comply with adversarial means. The war that has been within you is coming to an end. God is stepping up within you and He causes you to conquer the nature that rebels against His will for you. This is not your normal, it is a result of the past and trauma. But it will no longer prevail. It ends today.

I prophesy that today you are being strengthened to walk in total victory over your nature. Things that you call innate or genetic are all surrendering to the power of God within you. They will not be able to withstand the word of God over your life. You will prosper and be in good health.

1 John 5:9 - If we receive the witness of men, the witness of God is greater: for this is the witness of God which he hath testified of his Son.

NOVEMBER 22

Today is the day to receive the challenge of the lord to sow a seed that you have never sown before. You have been fearful of giving on the next level, but this seed will release you into another level of living. God has purposed it in your heart to give freely and liberally. Now is the time to exercise that purpose. You are earmarked to underwrite the kingdom through seeding. Today you welcome new challenges to give.

I prophesy to you today, that you search out new opportunities to sow into the kingdom of God. Not only will your seed be significant, but it will be like you've never sown before. I speak to your accounts that they will begin to make room for the bountiful harvest of wealth that is on its way to your house.

2 Corinthians 9:7 - Every man according as he purposeth in his heart, so let him give; not grudgingly, or of necessity: for God loveth a cheerful giver.

NOVEMBER 23

Today you will begin to see the seed of the lord fully matriculate and grow. You will bring forth the harvest full term. There will be no abortion or miscarriage of what has been placed inside you. The enemy has been trying to cause you to deliver prematurely, but not so. You will fully develop every assignment, ministry, destiny, vision and calling. It will come to pass full term and completely.

I prophesy to you today health, wealth and patience. The lord will cause you to birth forth what He has ordained for you. Do not fear or do not doubt. This will happen in the timing of God. I speak to your mind and your mouth that you speak only what the lord has said and you receive it with all your heart.

Isaiah 66:9 - Shall I bring to the birth, and not cause to bring forth? saith the Lord: shall I cause to bring forth, and shut the womb? saith thy God.

NOVEMBER 24

Today the Lord has placed you in the school of development and order. You have been chosen to carry out a priestly mandate. You can not avoid this any longer. You must embrace what has been set for you. This training will lead and guide you in the way to go. It will help you to see and understand clearly who you are and what you have been called to. Accept it once and for all. This is the doings of God.

Today I prophesy, that you allow yourself to be fully immersed in the plans of God for your life. I speak to your anointing and command it to hunger and thirst for development and training. As you endure this course and season you will matriculate to the servant of the lord that is needed in this hour.

Esther 4:14 - For if thou altogether holdest thy peace at this time, then shall there enlargement and deliverance arise to the Jews from another place; but thou and thy father's house shall be destroyed: and who knoweth whether thou art come to the kingdom for such a time as this?

NOVEMBER 25

Today grace will find you and not miss you. The grace of God has been given to you freely. Though you have felt that judgment has come to your door, the grace of God is your portion. You will not only receive the grace of God but it will be multiplied in your life. The things that resist this grace will be met with much judgment and fierceness. But grace has been sent from the heavens on your behalf and it will not stop until you are completely overtaken by it.

I prophesy to you today that you walk in the supernatural, multiplied grace of God. I speak to your mind and heart that you see life from a perspective of this grace. You will not miss it or will you lack it in any area. The grace of God is like no other and it is fully yours.

Acts 4:33 - And with great power gave the apostles witness of the resurrection of the Lord Jesus: and great grace was upon them all.

NOVEMBER 26

Today you will complete the work of God to become in the image of Jesus Christ. There has been resistance to this change and transformation. But it must be completed. Today you will endure the final phases to this completion. God has begun a great work within you to transform you into the image of His son. He will not stop until you resemble the pattern of Jesus Christ. This is why things are changing around you, because a holy transformation is taking place.

I prophesy that you are able to endure this spiritual metamorphosis. I speak to the fighter within you and command it to be dormant in this area. No longer will you resist this, but you will fully embrace it. I command every change that needs to take place to do so beginning today.

Romans 8:29 - For whom he did foreknow, he also did predestinate to be conformed to the image of his Son, that he might be the firstborn among many brethren.

NOVEMBER 27

Today is the day to intercede greatly for those of whom you desire to be saved. Family members, friends and acquaintances should be mentioned before the throne of God. Your prayers are being heard concerning their salvation. God's desire is to save them and set them free. He wants you to partner with Him and release from the earth, prayers that will agree with His will. You will see God's power to save the lost amongst those you pray for.

I prophesy to you today that you carry a burden for souls. I speak to your heart that it is tender towards those who do not know the lord. I prophesy that you will be compelled to witness and share the good news with those who may not know. You have been sent in the earth for this reason and today you will be greatly used of God.

Luke 19:10 - For the Son of man is come to seek and to save that which was lost.

NOVEMBER 28

Today you are being made more aware of your purpose in the earth. God is revealing to you what you have been sent to do and accomplish. Your heart has been searching for the things that are meant for you and meant for you to do. Today they are unfolding the more. You will see and know them. When they come, do not resist them or be in disbelief. It is the lord who will show them to you.

I prophesy today, that your eyes be open and your heart be prepared to receive the purpose of God for you. You will no longer ask the question 'why am I here?' for it will be revealed to you even today. I speak over your life that it walks in the perfect will of God. Today is the day of destiny.

Hebrews 13:21 - Make you perfect in every good work to do his will, working in you that which is well pleasing in his sight, through Jesus Christ; to whom be glory for ever and ever. Amen.

NOVEMBER 29

Today God causes your heart to be changed. You have been set on the old way of thinking and being, but there is a change that is taking place within you. This change is for your good. The eyes of your understanding must be opened and your perceptions must be adjusted. It is a godly change and it is good for you.

I prophesy to you today that you accept the transformation that is taking place in your mind and heart. It may be different from what you are used to, but it will please the lord as you allow the mind of Christ to overtake your mind. The lord gives you His heart today and it is better than your former heart.

Isaiah 65:17 - For, behold, I create new heavens and a new earth: and the former shall not be remembered, nor come into mind.

NOVEMBER 30

Today do not resist the call to consecration. The lord is calling you to Himself and He desires your attention. There is a meeting that you must make in the spirit. It will be a time of communion with God and a time of refreshing for you. This consecration will be ordained of God and He will lead you. Don't wait any longer. Put it in your schedule to meet the lord. He has things He desires to share with you.

I prophesy that today you will receive all that this consecration has for you. This will be a great time with the lord. I speak to your heart and spirit to be open to what He will share with you and how He will engage you. Allow the lord to minster to you. It will answer so many of your questions.

Isaiah 58:5 - Is it such a fast that I have chosen? a day for a man to afflict his soul? is it to bow down his head as a bulrush, and to spread sackcloth and ashes under him? wilt thou call this a fast, and an acceptable day to the Lord?

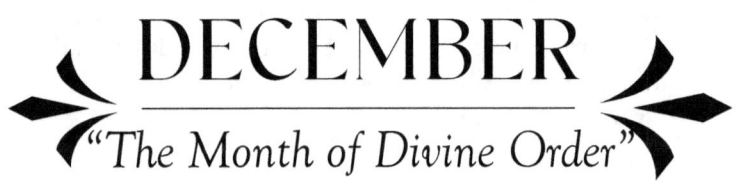

DECEMBER

"The Month of Divine Order"

DECEMBER 1

Today is the day for the divine order of God to be made manifested in your life. There are some things that the Lord has ordered and determined for you. You must begin to walk in them and allow them to unfold for you. God has set before you blessings. He desires that you welcome each blessing and prosper. Your plans will seem as though they are failing. But it is just an indication that everything God has not planned for you is falling to the ground. His plans will prevail.

I prophesy today, that you remain encouraged and uplifted. You have entered into a time that will seem like you will be betrayed, rejected and things will leave your life. This is not the enemy, but it is the Lord. He is causing everything that He has not ordered for you to be removed from you. Only His plan will succeed. Even the things you have chosen yourself, if they do not agree with His plans they will not manifest. But it is ok, what He has ordered is much better.

Proverbs 16:25 - There is a way that seemeth right unto a man, but the end thereof are the ways of death.

DECEMBER 2

Today is the day that you begin to witness the law of God in your life and those around you. The Lord God has decreed a great decree in your life and it sets precedence for the rest of your days. That decree is for you to prosper and be abundantly blessed. This new law sets boundaries to lack and poverty, that it can only come but so far to you. This law rebukes every devour that attempts to consume your wealth. God has set a law and it cannot be overturned.

Today I prophesy that you begin to live according to the law of God in your life to prosper you. May your mind begin to think and perceive wealth. May your ability to manage your finances increase so that you are a wealth builder and wealth manager. I agree with heaven concerning you and I speak to your life and command it to be governed by the decree of wealth.

Psalms 148:6 - He hath also stablished them for ever and ever: he hath made a decree which shall not pass.

DECEMBER 3

Today is the day that all of heaven moves in sync to establish you. You will see the workings of the fullness of God in your life. From creation, to redemption even to inspiration, it all will be the results of heaven moving in your life. New things are unfolding. Old things are returning with joy. And your eyes are being opened to new opportunities. This is what happens when heaven moves on your behalf.

I prophesy to you today, that you live a life that flows with the course of God. I speak to every stagnant place and command it to be unstuck. I speak to every difficult place and command it to be made easy. You will prosper. You have been chosen to prosper. I speak this over you and within you.

1 John 5:7 - For there are three that bear record in heaven, the Father, the Word, and the Holy Ghost: and these three are one.

DECEMBER 4

Today God takes authority over your path. The enemy has been working overtime to detour you from the way of the Lord. He has been trying to get you off course. But he will not prevail. You have even worked against yourself by allowing distractions to cause you to venture off into undesired directions. But today, God takes authority over it all. He orders your steps and lightens your path. He guides you with His eye.

Today, I prophesy that you are sensitive to the leading of the Lord. May your discernment be sharpened and your ability to pivot be sure. God is turning you to a new direction and it is the way of peace, joy and triumph. Trust His plans and trust His ways. It will benefit you in every way.

Psalms 32:8 - I will instruct thee and teach thee in the way which thou shalt go: I will guide thee with mine eye.

DECEMBER 5

Today God proclaims the law of grace and favor in your life. This proclamation causes you to walk into blessings that you have not earned or warranted. God has determined to do this thing for you. You will begin to inherit things that were supposed to pass you, but God stopped it at your door. He has announced your life to be favored in every way. All of heaven and earth has heard Him and today they all begin to comply with this divine proclamation.

I prophesy that today you come into full agreement with God and His decision to favor you. His kindness towards you, reflects His thoughts about you. May you see yourself as God sees you. I speak over your heart and command it to be prepared to be overwhelmed by God's loving grace and favor.

Esther 2:17 - the king loved Esther more than all the women, and she won grace and favor in his sight more than all the virgins, so that he set the royal crown on her head and made her queen instead of Vashti.

DECEMBER 6

Today is the day that those who are assigned to bless you are released to do so. God has many ways of blessing you and He has earmarked people in the earth that will participate in getting the blessing to you. Even strangers will be led to do you favors. They may not be aware why they are doing it, but the Lord has commanded them to bless you. Your blessing will come from people near and far. Expect the calls, emails and notifications today. The blessing will be arriving soon.

I prophesy to you today that you begin to squash all your prejudices and hang-ups concerning people. Those same people will be used of God to come and bless your life. May you be healed from the past and delivered from yesterday so that your tomorrows will shine bright as the noonday sun. I command you to be open today to the people God will use.

Luke 6:38 - Give, and it shall be given unto you; good measure, pressed down, and shaken together, and running over, shall men give into your bosom. For with the same measure that ye mete withal it shall be measured to you again.

DECEMBER 7

Today is the day that you experience God settling issues and old matters. You will begin to see the Lord resolve things that were left undone and incomplete. Today will be a day of closure and completion. The Lord has orchestrated this for you and He is involved in every detail of finalizing matters that concern you. Be prepared to walk in a whole place in life.

I prophesy to you today that you embrace the completion of old matters. Do not return to the old place or the old mindset. It is finished and complete. May you begin to allow God to close old doors and windows so that new ones may open to you. It all begins today for you.

Isaiah 58:12 - And they that shall be of thee shall build the old waste places: thou shalt raise up the foundations of many generations; and thou shalt be called, The repairer of the breach, The restorer of paths to dwell in.

DECEMBER 8

Today God arranges a new start for you. It's your "do it again" season. The Lord God is rewriting your story and allowing you to participate in the development of your testimony. Your life will not end until the blessing has completely overtaken you. You will be graced to start again, but this time it will be with the complete influence of God.

I prophesy to you today that you walk in your new start. I speak boldness upon you to take a step forward into what is now made available for you. I command you to be free from the past and move into your next even NOW! I prophetically declare that you are now in your new season.

Deuteronomy 11:14 - That I will give you the rain of your land in his due season, the first rain and the latter rain, that thou mayest gather in thy corn, and thy wine, and thine oil.

DECEMBER 9

Today God brings into order your breakthrough. He causes the things that were hindering you and holding you back to be loosed from your life. God begins to settle all chaotic behaviors and environments that cause you anxiety and discomfort. God has ordered the atmosphere to agree with you purpose and to reveal His glory upon your life.

Today I prophesy to you that you begin to walk in your breakthrough. I speak over your entire life that every part of it is in agreement with what God says about you. I speak to your mind, your will and your emotions that they all comply with the holy revolution that is presently occurring. You will no longer be bound. You are being made free today.

Matthew 6:20 - But lay up for yourselves treasures in heaven, where neither moth nor rust doth corrupt, and where thieves do not break through nor steal:

DECEMBER 10

Today is the day that the government of heaven and your will meet. Not only is God influencing all your decisions, but also you are beginning to operate in total alignment with what He decides. There is a divine agreement with heaven and earth occurring in your life today. You will make all the right decisions and God will impact each of them.

I prophesy to you today that you yield yourself and your members to the leading of the Lord. May you completely surrender to the will of God and discover all that He has decided for you. Your agreement will release you into another level of revelation and understanding concerning the things of God.

Proverbs 2:6 - For the Lord giveth wisdom: out of his mouth cometh knowledge and understanding.

DECEMBER 11

Today is the day that God commands your feet to firm and your steps to be sure. You will not be swayed on matters that are not in agreement with what God has already determined over your life. You will walk with a resolve like never before. There is a holy stubbornness that comes upon you. The enemy will not be able to move you from this conviction.

I prophesy to you today that you become more bold and assured in who and what you believe. I speak over your mind and will that it becomes convicted when the spirit of compromise is present. You will not be moved by winds, doctrines or theories that pull you out of the will of God. Today stand firm and remain there until the Lord says different.

Proverbs 4:27 - Turn not to the right hand nor to the left: remove thy foot from evil.

DECEMBER 12

Today you will experience God making the enemy of your soul obey His instructions. You will discover that God is in charge and He controls all creatures. Yes, even the devil has to submit to the order of God. Today God commands satan and his demons to retreat and back up from any attack. Your faith has been sharpened and your strength has increased. Your enemy will not be able to prevail. God has ordered him to cease and desist.

I prophesy to you today that you simply trust in the strength and the order of God over your life. Heaven rules over your life and affairs and God has caused demonic activity to stop. May you walk in confidence in the power of God. May your eyes be focused on the Lord and receive what He is doing. I command you to agree with God in all things and you will see blessings unfold.

Job 13:18 - Behold now, I have ordered my cause;
I know that I shall be justified.

DECEMBER 13

Today is the day that you cease from rebelling against God's decisions for your life. You will begin to embrace all that the Lord had decided for you. You will no longer fight against His will or His word concerning you. There is another "Yes Lord" rising from within you. Your will begins to die with the will of God and you accept it as your own.

Today I prophesy to you that the fight in you against the things of God dies. There is a holy mandate over your life and you must accept it. As you do this, you will discover new levels of peace and serenity. You will walk in new realms of victory and triumph. I speak to your will that rebels against God to cease. May your flesh be crucified so that your purpose may live.

Job 24:13 - They are of those that rebel against the light; they know not the ways thereof, nor abide in the paths thereof.

DECEMBER 14

Today the Lord decides to Passover your shortcomings and error in order to grant you the grace of His mercy. Because the Lord is the righteous judge, He decides that you are worth your future. He will not even allow you to invade your own purpose. God has overlooked your wrongdoings and gives you another opportunity to please Him in all of your ways. Take full advantage of this merciful season.

I prophesy to you today that you do not attempt to justify any of your wrongdoings, but rather you repent and be honest before the lord. He has already determined to bless you and will give you what you need. May you fully embrace this grace and enjoy the benefits it employs. I speak over your heart that it desires to please God no matter what it takes.

Genesis 18:32 - And he said, Oh let not the Lord be angry, and I will speak yet but this once: Peradventure ten shall be found there. And he said, I will not destroy it for ten's sake.

DECEMBER 15

Today is the day to settle in the order of God for your life. The season of an unsettling is over for you. You have been anxious and discontented with so many things. You have been boggled down with burdens that do not belong to you. But today you are being removed from that place and being sat down in the order of God for your life.

I prophesy to you today that you being to rest in what God allows. Permit the lord to do a work in you that will calm your fears and smooth all your doubts. God is in control and I speak to your heart to believe and trust His power. You are under heavens jurisdiction and you are being positioned to give Him greater glory.

Habakkuk 1:5 - Behold ye among the heathen, and regard, and wonder marvellously: for I will work a work in your days, which ye will not believe, though it be told you.

DECEMBER 16

Today Gods order of Love reigns in your heart. There is a new rule and government that is taking charge in your life. The ruler is given an order to shift you from chaos to peace. The rule of Love is given a responsibility to bring you into a place of contentment and faith. You will not be consumed by hatred or forgiveness. Love will not allow it. There is no longer room for it within you.

Today I prophesy to you that you being to comply with the new order and government that God has allowed. This is not just any order, it is the order of God. May your heart be renewed and your spirit be strengthened. It is a new day for you.

Colossians 3:15 - And let the peace of God rule in your hearts, to the which also ye are called in one body; and be ye thankful.

DECEMBER 17

Today you are being aligned with the fullness of God's purpose for you. The Lord has preordained your future and calling. Life has taken a toll on you and the enemy of your soul has attempted to misalign you from that purpose. But today God has moved things in order and caused them to agree with what He has already determined. Do not fear or fret when things and people begin to move. The Lord is putting things in place.

I prophesy to you today that you begin to trust God in all things. It will seem like you are loosing, but really you are gaining. The Lord is putting things in order so that you life may be fully aligned. May you lean in to the heart if God through prayer and fasting so that you are sensitive to His desires for you. I speak to your heart that it be guarded from hurt, pain and disappointment. Greater is ahead for you.

Proverbs 3:5 - Trust in the Lord with all thine heart; and lean not unto thine own understanding.

DECEMBER 18

Today you will know the Lord in a new way. Revelation will be opened to you so that you may worship the Lord, as you have never known Him before. Jesus said that He is the Way, the Truth and the Life. Today you will know Him as LIFE! His life will affect your life and His life becomes your life. You are being enlightened as never before to live the life that He has ordained for you.

I prophesy to you today that you being to breath in the life of God; the life that He intends for you. The Lord, who is life, makes your life more fulfilled and complete. So today I say LIVE! Live Gods life. Live the life of Jesus and you will see what great things will unfold for you.

John 14:6 - Jesus saith unto him, I am the way, the truth, and the life: no man cometh unto the Father, but by me.

DECEMBER 19

Today the Lord has commanded your life to be completely changed for His Glory. God has made a decision concerning you and His decision is greatest for you. The Lord has taken over the affairs and orders of your life. You simply have to agree with what He has determined. Divine order is your mandate and blessing. Your life is falling under the order of God.

I prophesy to you today that you begin to submit to the order of God. Begin to elevate your prayers and thinking. God has a higher call and purpose for you. May your vision for your life increase so that it matches what God says about you. Greater is for you and you must see it and speak it over yourself daily.

1 Corinthians 2:9 - But as it is written, Eye hath not seen, nor ear heard, neither have entered into the heart of man, the things which God hath prepared for them that love him.

DECEMBER 20

Today the Lord God has completed a cycle in your life. You have been in a series of testing to determine your readiness for your next. Today God has said yes to your future and everything that is for you. Your future calls for you today because your previous level has been completed. This is an elevation for you in life.

I prophesy to you today that you begin to prepare for what is next. May you open your heart for the new things that will begin to unfold for you. I speak to your whole being that you begin to shift to the next place that has already been determined yours.

Daniel 1:20 - And in all matters of wisdom and understanding, that the king enquired of them, he found them ten times better than all the magicians and astrologers that were in all his realm.

DECEMBER 21

Today the Lord God takes authority over the wickedness that has come to you. There has been many adversarial attacks coming to you that has hindered you and held you back. But today, Heaven has not just waged war against it, but God has taken over their orders. He commands principalities and powers to move back from you and cease their attacks. God has spoken to all darkness and wickedness and commanded them to move.

I prophesy to you today that you begin to rejoice and be glad. The Lord has determined the victory shall come to your house and your life. This order of cease and desist has released victory upon you. So all you must do is rejoice because the darkness is being expelled and the attacks will be no longer for a season.

Isaiah 45:22 - Look unto me, and be ye saved, all the ends of the earth: for I am God, and there is none else.

DECEMBER 22

Today God is managing your happiness. Your desire to be happy has been heard in heaven. The Lord is releasing atmospheres of joy in your direction. Buckets of laughter and glee will be your portion. Cheerfulness will be your new normal. You will dwell in a mental and emotional place that is most pleasurable.

I prophesy to you today that your soul will be in delight at all times. Even when times are challenging, you will be at peace and will be able to discover joy in the midst of it. May your days be bright. May your weeks be filled with bliss. I speak pleasure over your entire life.

Psalms 128:2 - For thou shalt eat the labour of thine hands: happy shalt thou be, and it shall be well with thee.

DECEMBER 23

Today God is birthing a new desire within you to do His will. There has been a burden growing within you to be a world changer. You have been feeling a pull to affect the communities and people around you. That burden has matriculated into a mandate to move forward. Lives are waiting to be touched by you. You will make a mark that will never be forgotten.

I prophesy to you today that you give birth to this new thing. It has been growing and is now time to release it from within you. It is time for you to walk in the fullness of your calling. I speak to your anointing and command it to intensify. I speak to the oil upon your life and I declare that it will flow and not be hindered so that you may affect the lives that are around you.

Ezekiel 17:8 - It was planted in a good soil by great waters, that it might bring forth branches, and that it might bear fruit, that it might be a goodly vine.

DECEMBER 24

Today you will be brought into a new order and sequence of divine structure. The Lord has commanded that you be brought into a new realm of construction and growth. This will release the answers to your prayers and confirm all that you have dealt with in the last couple of months. This year will not close without you being shifted into this new priestly course that God has ordered for you.

I prophesy to you today that your eyes be opened to see what the Lord is revealing to you. I speak to your heart that is doesn't dwell in fear but rather that you will believe God for what He is doing in this new season. You're being constructed fro your next season. You're being built to last.

1 Peter 2:5 - Ye also, as lively stones, are built up a spiritual house, an holy priesthood, to offer up spiritual sacrifices, acceptable to God by Jesus Christ.

DECEMBER 25

Today, the celebration of the birth of Christ is a testimony of the multiplied grace that has come to you. As the wise men that went to meet the Christ child were blessed by His coming, so will you be abundantly blessed by His presence with you. You are being enveloped in the joy of Christmas and the wealth of favor that comes to you in this season.

I prophesy to you today that you begin to walk in and live in this grace. I speak to every area of your life that is flows with favor and that you have new opportunities of increase. May your life be filled with jubilant peace and good will. As you open your hand to give and sow, so will the blessings of heaven flow into your life.

Isaiah 9:6 - For unto us a child is born, unto us a son is given: and the government shall be upon his shoulder: and his name shall be called Wonderful, Counsellor, The mighty God, The everlasting Father, The Prince of Peace.

DECEMBER 26

Today you are coming into the fullness of the revelation that God has created you in His image. The Lord God has decided to form you and shape you in His likeness and your understanding of this is crucial to the days ahead of you. As you begin to embrace this divine attribute of yours, you will begin to take authority over the things that occur in your life. This revelation will birth a new perspective within you, which will benefit you greatly.

I prophesy to you today that you begin to walk in this divine image, knowing that you not only belong to God but you are created in His image. I speak over your entire being that you begin to live out this nature and formation.

Genesis 1:26 - And God said, Let us make man in our image, after our likeness: and let them have dominion over the fish of the sea, and over the fowl of the air, and over the cattle, and over all the earth, and over every creeping thing that creepeth upon the earth.

DECEMBER 27

Today the Lord has ordered you to walk in another realm of sanctification. This year cannot close unless you make certain sacrifices and steps towards your holy purpose. The next year is going to be one of your greatest years in your life. You must prepare your spirit now. There must be a greater commitment to the things of God so that you are prepared to serve Him in spite of anything.

Today I prophesy to you that you recommit your soul to the Lord. This renewal of your salvation will refresh your soul and heart into the new things that the Lord will reveal to you. As you consider your ways and make the necessary adjustments, the Holy Spirit will give you the grace to do it and maintain it. It all is a prerequisite for your next level.

Ephesians 4:23 - And be renewed in the spirit of your mind;

DECEMBER 28

Today God has arranged your environments and atmospheres to yield to you fruit. You will see the hand of God on your life as if things are perfectly set up for you. You will walk in perfect timing, perfect purpose, perfect connections and perfect resources. God has prescribed this for you and it will bring you into new realms of productivity. You will be fruitful like never before.

I prophesy to you today that you be at peace with what is happening with you and trust God to control it all. I speak to your will that you agree completely with the things that God is doing. May you embrace the perfection in the earth that belongs to you. It may not seem perfect when you look at it with your natural eyes, but in the spirit you will see the precision that God has orchestrated.

2 Samuel 22:33 - God is my strength and power:
and he maketh my way perfect.

DECEMBER 29

Today the Lord God has prepared a change for you. He has not changed His mind concerning you, but you must change in order to receive what is next for you. It is just a few more days until the next year for you and there are key changes in your life that must tale place. The Lord God has made a decision for you to adjust the things that need adjusting. These alterations are tailor made for your future and it fits you precisely.

I prophesy to you today that you welcome the changes that God has ordered for you. Change is good and you need to embrace it for your next. These changes may be challenging at first but you will settle into it quickly. God will be with you through it and He will guide you with His spirit. Trust God and make the changes.

Job 14:14 - If a man die, shall he live again? all the days of my appointed time will I wait, till my change come.

DECEMBER 30

Today the Lord is calling you on a final consecration for this year. He desires to show you what is to come for the next year and give you the marching orders for your life. The Lord wants to share with you the previews of what is to come. Your level of consecration will increase as you set yourself aside for the use of the lord today.

I prophesy to you today that you yield to the Spirit of Grace and set yourself apart from the rest of the world for the one last time of this year. May you be sensitive in your ear to hear what the spirit of the Lord is saying to you. May you be discerning in your spirit to sense what the Lord is downloading within you. May your soul be light so that you are divinely aware of the leading of the lord. There will be much that He will share with you.

Exodus 28:3 - And thou shalt speak unto all that are wise hearted, whom I have filled with the spirit of wisdom, that they may make Aaron's garments to consecrate him, that he may minister unto me in the priest's office.

DECEMBER 31

Today is the last day of the year. God will have you to settle in His name. Your future has already been determined. Your purpose has been etched out of time and God has decided that the days ahead are good. All you must do is settle in the identity of God. As you do so you will be prepared for next year.

I prophesy to you today that wealth and prosperity will be your portion. You will receive supernatural favor and blessings from all directions will come to find you and overtake you. The last day of this year will be the first day of your new beginning. Even before the clock strikes twelve the abundance of Gods favor will already be upon you. You and your whole household will be safe.

Proverbs 18:10 - The name of the Lord is a strong tower: the righteous runneth into it, and is safe.